Walter and Ingrid Trobisch and the Globalization of Modern, Christian Sexual Ethics

Walter and Ingrid Trobisch and the Globalization of Modern, Christian Sexual Ethics

ANNEKE H. STASSON

☙PICKWICK *Publications* · Eugene, Oregon

WALTER AND INGRID TROBISCH AND THE GLOBALIZATION OF MODERN, CHRISTIAN SEXUAL ETHICS

Copyright © 2021 Anneke H. Stasson. All rights reserved. Except for brief quotations in critical publications or reviews, no part of this book may be reproduced in any manner without prior written permission from the publisher. Write: Permissions, Wipf and Stock Publishers, 199 W. 8th Ave., Suite 3, Eugene, OR 97401.

Some content from the introduction and chapter 3 were previously published as "Modern Marital Practices and the Growth of World Christianity during the Mid-Twentieth Century." *Church History: Studies in Christianity and Culture* 84.2 (June 2015). Reprinted with permission.

Pickwick Publications
An Imprint of Wipf and Stock Publishers
199 W. 8th Ave., Suite 3
Eugene, OR 97401

www.wipfandstock.com

PAPERBACK ISBN: 978-1-7252-5397-1
HARDCOVER ISBN: 978-1-7252-5398-8
EBOOK ISBN: 978-1-7252-5399-5

Cataloguing-in-Publication data:

Names: Stasson, Anneke H.

Title: Walter and Ingrid Trobisch and the globalization of modern, Christian sexual ethics / Anneke H. Stasson.

Description: Eugene, OR: Pickwick Publications, 2021 | Includes bibliographical references.

Identifiers: ISBN 978-1-7252-5397-1 (paperback) | ISBN 978-1-7252-5398-8 (hardcover) | ISBN 978-1-7252-5399-5 (ebook)

Subjects: LCSH: Trobisch, Walter. | Trobisch, Ingrid Hult. | Sex—Religious aspects—Christianity. | Sexual ethics. | Marriage—Religious aspects—Christianity. | Globalization—Religious aspects—Christianity.

Classification: BT708 S73 2021 (paperback) | BT708 (ebook)

05/12/21

Contents

Acknowledgments	vii
Introduction	1
1 | Pioneer Missionaries in Tcholliré, Cameroon	9
2 | Composing *J'ai Aimé Une Fille* at Cameroon Christian College in Libamba	33
3 | Marriage Counseling by Mail from the Austrian Alps	54
4 | Leaders in a Christian Home Movement in Africa	70
5 | "Reverse Mission" among American Evangelicals	96
Conclusion: The Trobisches as Shapers of Global, Christian Sexual Ethics in the Mid-Twentieth Century	121
Bibliography	131

Acknowledgments

I want to thank my mentor and friend Dr. Dana Robert for her inspiring research and wise counsel. I am grateful for a grant from the Lilly Endowment, which supported my research. I received helpful feedback from members of the Theological Research Seminar and the John Wesley Honors College at Indiana Wesleyan University. Thanks go to David and Stephen Trobisch for meeting with me back in 2010, for their warm hospitality, and for making available their mother's papers. I hope they find this study of their parents acceptable. I want to thank my own parents, Mark and Sandra Spee, for cultivating a truly Christian home, for raising their children to be curious about the world and faithful to its Creator. I could not have completed this project without the Mary Poppins of my life, Robin Bakken. And what's Mary Poppins without Bert—so thanks, Virgil, for all the fun you bring to our family. And thanks, Grandpa Steve, for your excitement and encouragement as I've worked on this project. Thanks go to my four beautiful children, Mary Lou, Eleanor, Ruthann, and Joseph, who each fill me with joy and give me new insight into what it means to be a child of God. Above all, I want to thank my husband Stevie for accompanying me on this journey of discovering what Ingrid Trobisch meant when she said, "The family is the best landing place for the gospel."

Introduction

In 1962, Walter Trobisch, a missionary of German ethnicity working in Cameroon for the American Lutheran Church, published a book for young Africans on love, sex, and marriage. Trobisch described his book as "a pamphlet against the bride-price and a plea for the beauty of marital love."[1] He called the book *J'ai Aimé Une Fille* (*I Loved a Girl*) and wrote the book as a series of letters between himself and a hypothetical former student, whom he called François. It opened with an angry letter from François, who had just been fired from his teaching position for having premarital sex: "Last Friday, I loved a girl—or, as you would put it, I committed adultery—at least that's what the whites call it and the Church, too."[2] François believed he was blameless since "the girl wasn't married, nor had any bride-price been paid for her." Trobisch responded in a letter arguing that "sexual union fulfills its purpose only when it is an expression of love." He then elaborated on his view of love:

> You did not love that girl; you went to bed with her—these are two completely different things. You had a sexual episode, but what love is, you did not experience. . . . Let me try to tell you what it really should mean if a fellow says to a girl, 'I love you.' It means: 'You, you, you. You alone. You shall reign in my heart. . . . I will give everything for you and I will give up everything for you . . . I want to share with you my thoughts, my heart and my body—all that I possess. I want to listen to what you have to say. There is nothing I want to undertake without your blessing. I want to remain always at your side.[3]

---

1. Trobisch, "Courtship without Dating," 4.
2. Trobisch, *Complete Works of Walter Trobisch*, 31.
3. Trobisch, *Complete Works of Walter Trobisch*, 33–34.

As the book progresses, François meets a young woman on a bus (Cecile), falls in love with her, and the two begin to make plans to be married. However, their dreams are dashed when Cecile's father demands a bride-price of four hundred dollars. The story ends with a letter from François, bitterly decrying the bride-price system and the fact that Trobisch has led him to a dead end: "Four hundred dollars! For me this is altogether out of the question, an impossible amount. You have made me dream. But reality is cruel and destroys that dream. I've ceased to hope."[4]

Despite the tragic ending, or perhaps, as Trobisch argued, because of the tragic ending, *I Loved a Girl* was wildly popular in Africa. Between 1962 and 1965, 30,000 copies of the book were sold in French Cameroon alone. Translations existed or were in progress for about thirty African languages. Within a decade 1 million copies of *I Loved a Girl* were in circulation, and it was available in seventy different languages.[5]

When twenty-one-year-old C. Tanmi of Cameroon read Trobisch's book, she was shocked at the extent to which the story mirrored her own. She wrote to Trobisch, "The whole book seems to be dealing with my personal difficulties." Tanmi was "in love with a class-mate" of hers, but was engaged to a man her parents had chosen for her. "When I was only 17 my parents influence me to like a certain young man," she wrote. "It was later decided that we should become married in future but sorry that I have not even a grain of love for this young man."[6]

In 1965, Tanmi's letter was one of a thousand letters that Trobisch had received from people in twenty different African countries. Because Trobisch wrote *I Loved a Girl* as a series of letters and included his own address on the back cover, readers like Tanmi wasted no time in writing to him for advice about the relational issues in their own lives. Trobisch and his wife Ingrid started an impromptu counseling service by mail, which they called Marriage Guidance Service for Africa. In 1971, Ingrid Trobisch told a friend, "We have received about 7000 letters from 32 different African countries."[7] Most of these letters were written in French or English. Today between four and five thousand of these letters are housed in the archives of the Evangelical Lutheran Church in America. The letters reveal how some young people in mid-twentieth-century Africa were wrestling with sexual and marital changes wrought by industrialization, urbanization, colonial

---

4. Trobisch, *Complete Works of Walter Trobisch*, 57.

5. Melvin Arnold to I. Trobisch, 13 June 1969, Ingrid Trobisch Papers, "Family Life Mission," May 1973, Missionary Personnel Files.

6. C. Tanmi to W. Trobisch, June 1965, Walter Trobisch Collection, Box 15, Folder T.

7. I. Trobisch to Mrs. Johnson, 25 August 1971, Walter Trobisch Collection, Box 19.

encounters, and new forms of education. Because many of the Africans who wrote to Trobisch were Christians who had thoroughly embraced modern marital practices like spouse self-selection, marrying for love, and companionate marriage, the letters also offer insight into the correlation between Christianity and the rise of these modern martial ideals.

The letters alone make the Trobisches' story worth hearing, but also interesting is the fact that the book Trobisch wrote for Africa ended up being quite popular in the United States as well. In 1964, the evangelical campus ministry InterVarsity Christian Fellowship published an English edition of *I Loved a Girl* in its flagship magazine, *HIS*. In response, Trobisch received yet another stream of letters, this time from American college students, who were themselves wrestling with how to live as Christians in the midst of the sexual revolution. As a young reader from Wisconsin wrote in her letter to Trobisch, "Premarital relations are a major point of discussion and concern among students today. Rarely is a strong, articulate word such as this spoken for the standards God has set for us."[8] The letters to the Trobisches reveal the ways in which young people around the world—particularly Christian young people—were negotiating sexual ethics in the midst of rapid social change in the mid-twentieth century.

THE GLOBAL LOVE REVOLUTION

The letters to the Trobisches and, indeed, the Trobisches' entire story must be situated in the context of the reevaluation of sexual and marital practices that took place between the eighteenth and the twentieth centuries. In the eighteenth century, the industrial revolution, urbanization, and new forms of Protestantism led to changes in family relations in Europe and North America. As young people moved away from family farms and settled in towns to work in factories, their ties to extended kin decreased. Many of these individuals were also affected by what Lawrence Stone has called the "affective individualism" of Puritanism.[9] These young people began to choose their own spouse and marry for love. Whereas marriage had once been the purview of the state and the church, the Enlightenment challenged traditional sources of authority like the king and the church, effectively making marriage more of a private affair and less of a public institution. Moreover, the criticism of monarchy led in turn to the criticism of hierarchy in marriage. When combined with the gains of the women's rights movement in the early twentieth century—suffrage and more educational and

---

8. W. and I. Trobisch to friends, September 1964, Missionary Personnel Files.
9. Stone, *Family, Sex, and Marriage in England*, 224–25.

professional opportunities for women—these factors successfully transformed Western marriage from a family affair with economic and political concerns to a personal choice based on love. Stephanie Coontz has called this transformation a "love revolution."[10]

In the 1960s, sociologist William Goode was the first to draw attention to the global nature of this love revolution.

> For the first time in world history a common set of influences— the social forces of industrialization and urbanization—is affecting every known society. Even traditional family systems in such widely separate and diverse societies as Papua, Manus, China, and Yugoslavia are reported to be changing as a result of these forces, although at different rates of speed. The alteration seems to be in the direction of some type of *conjugal* family pattern—that is, toward fewer kinship ties with distant relatives and a greater emphasis on the 'nuclear' family unity of couple and children.[11]

As kinship ties loosened around the world and young people struck out on their own, other changes in family relations ensued. Young couples began expecting their marriages to be marked by a greater sense of intimacy and partnership than was present in the marriages of their parents.[12] And if their marriages proved unsatisfactory, these young couples were more likely to divorce than their parents' generation had been, such that by the mid-twentieth century divorce was on the rise globally.[13]

Gender relations were particularly in flux for twentieth-century women in industrializing nations. Increasingly, these women had access to education and professional employment.[14] Education cultivated a sense of individualism and fostered an identity apart from that which came from being a wife and mother. Higher education also gave women skills that might enable them to obtain a relatively well-paying job. The money they earned allowed women who had once been dependent on fathers and husbands for financial support to support themselves. Women who were occupied with gaining a higher education or holding down a well-paying job could postpone marriage and motherhood or forgo these things altogether. Those women who did marry often had fewer children than their own mothers.[15]

10. Coontz, *Marriage, a History*, 143.
11. Goode, *World Revolution and Family Patterns*, 1.
12. Lloyd, *Africa in Social Change*, 30.
13. Goode, *World Revolution and Family Patterns*, 9, 81–86, 262–63, 315–18.
14. Goode, *World Revolution and Family Patterns*, 21.
15. Goode, *World Revolution and Family Patterns*, 337–41.

In sum, global gender relations during the mid-twentieth century were beginning to be marked by a greater sense of personal choice.[16] When and whom to marry, whether to get a divorce, whether to seek paid employment, how many children to have—in previous generations, these questions had been answered in consultation with one's family. By the mid-twentieth century, however, individual men and women were beginning to make their own decisions about marriage and parenthood.

Although societies around the world were moving in the direction of the conjugal model of family, this shift was not a smooth one. Cultural chasms often developed between the young, who were open to new sexual norms, and the old, who insisted on preserving cultural traditions like the bride-price and arranged marriage.[17] The young did have more freedom to shape their own futures, but that new freedom had its own constraints. Previous generations knew what was expected of them. They knew what it meant to be a man or a woman, they knew what marriage would be like, and they knew that having children was the central purpose of marriage. Moreover, as they entered each phase of life they knew that there would be elders and kin to guide them. As young people began to stretch traditional definitions of marriage and gender relations, they often despaired at the inability of kin to understand and advise them. The social confusion caused by global changes in gender relations and martial practices formed the context for the enthusiastic reception of the Trobisches' message about love, sex, and marriage.

MISSION, COLONIALISM, AND SEXUALITY IN AFRICA

Much of the scholarship on Christian mission, colonialism, and sexuality in Africa has highlighted the intrusive, oppressive quality of Western sexual ethics. In an article about family life in South Africa, Sylvia Moena has argued, "The Christian gospel became a destructive agent used to propagate the expansion of capitalism or cultural imperialism."[18] John and Jean Comaroff have argued that missionaries were especially successful in enforcing their model of family because they were able to colonize consciousness: "The European colonization of Africa was often less a directly coercive conquest than a persuasive attempt to colonize consciousness, to remake people

---

16. Goode, *World Revolution and Family Patterns*, 380.

17. The problematic nature of the term "bride-price" is noted in the discussion of John Mbiti in chapter 4. However, "bride-price" will be used throughout this study because it was the term most commonly used during the era under investigation.

18. Moena, "Family Life in Soweto," 255.

by redefining the taken-for-granted surfaces of their everyday worlds."[19] Modupe Labode has described the oppressive atmosphere of mission schools for girls in South Africa, where girls would occasionally revolt against the school's program for them, which included being indoctrinated with the virtues of "purity and integrity, humility and industry" and participating in a grueling training regimen of "laundry, housework, and cookery."[20] Fiona Bowie has said that most missionaries "were as arrogant in their enforcement of monogamy as they were blind to the benefits offered by institutionalized polygyny."[21]

In some ways, the Trobisches' story confirms this narrative. By their presence in Africa—introducing Western goods, medicine, and technology, negotiating with colonial governments, working with a mission that established an industrial school—the Trobisches helped to facilitate colonialism, both in ways they perceived and lamented and in ways that escaped their knowledge. Like other missionaries of their era, the Trobisches failed to understand the nuances of local marital customs. They did not fully grasp how their "Christian" marital ideals were as much a product of changes in the economic structure of Western society as they were a translation of biblical ideals. And on several occasions, Walter Trobisch crossed the boundary between offering advice and imposing his views on his African students and colleagues.

However, the Trobisches' story also offers new perspectives on the complex relationship among Christian mission, colonialism, and sexuality in Africa. For the most part, the dynamic that unfolds in the letters young Africans wrote to Trobisch is not one of "colonizer and colonized," "imposition and response," or "hegemony and resistance."[22] Rather, the letters to Trobisch reveal a conversation. The letters demonstrate the ways in which African women and men were using Christian teaching on sexuality to make sense of their experience of growing up in modern, urban Africa.

Given that it was the era of African nationalism, the "moratorium" on foreign missions, and the birth of African theology—movements that sought African independence from the West—one would expect readers of *I Loved a Girl* to express some pushback against Trobisch's advocacy of marital practices that many considered to be "Western."[23] However, the

19. Comaroff and Comaroff, *Of Revelation and Revolution*, 313.
20. Labode, "From Heathen Kraal to Christian Home," 129, 132.
21. Bowie, "Elusive Christian Family," 146.
22. Hunt, "Introduction," 4.
23. My survey of the material found only one person who expressed any kind of criticism of Trobisch's view of love, sex, and marriage. The letter came from S. Iyoku, a 25-year-old preacher and Bible translator in Nigeria. Interestingly, Iyoku's criticism

letters to Trobisch give no sense that readers found these marital practices to be antithetical to either nationalism or the indigenization of Christianity in Africa. Neither did they feel that spouse self-selection and marrying for love somehow impinged upon their African identity. On the contrary, most believed these practices enabled them to more fully express their identity as modern Africans. They found these practices to be in line with their desire for political independence. The process of spouse self-selection also proved for many to be a means of deepening their Christian faith.

Another element in the Trobisches' story that complicates the conventional mission and colonialism narrative is the way in which the Trobisches conducted "mission in reverse." As their experience in Africa made them critical about certain trends in the West, such as racism and the neglect of home life, they did not hesitate to bring these critiques to the churches that hosted them on furlough and to the missionaries they interacted with on the field. Moreover, as the Trobisches developed a thriving counseling ministry with American evangelicals, they encouraged these evangelicals to adopt African perspectives on femininity, fertility, childbirth, and breastfeeding. Thus, the Trobisches were as much conduits for the global flow of critiques, ideologies, and practices from Africa to the West as they were implicated in the colonialist legacy in Africa. Ultimately, the Trobisches' vision of love, sex, and marriage helped both American and African Christians to navigate changing sexual norms of the mid-twentieth century.

CHAPTER OUTLINE

Chapter 1 describes how the Trobisches' interest in marriage and gender relations was piqued in the early 1950s as they interacted with African couples as pioneer missionaries in Tcholliré, Cameroon. Chapter 2 tells of their second missionary term in Cameroon, when Walter served as chaplain and professor of German and Bible at Cameroon Christian College in Libamba. At this point, he and Ingrid began to invest deeply in sexual and marital counseling with the student population at Libamba. Walter's *J'ai Aimé Une Fille* (published in 1962) and Ingrid's *On Our Way Rejoicing* (published in 1964) facilitated the Trobisches' transition out of Africa and into new forms of mission. They began to direct more of their time to writing books and answering the letters that came to them from people who had read their books.

---

was that Trobisch was too lenient on African traditions like polygamy (S. Iyoku to W. Trobisch, 2 January 1972).

Chapter 3 describes the work of Marriage Guidance Service for Africa (MGSA), the organization the Trobisches founded when they moved from Cameroon to the Lichtenberg, a region of the Austrian Alps. The letters they received demonstrate that young people in Africa had largely embraced modern marital practices like spouse self-selection and marrying for love, but they struggled with specific questions like, "How do I choose a spouse?" These young people appreciated Trobisch's practical advice and his suggestions for relating sexuality to Christian faith.

Chapter 4 relates the work of MGSA to a wider Christian home movement that had been building in Africa since the 1930s. During the 1960s the Trobisches were instrumental in popularizing this movement. They also shaped the theological discussion about the Christian home in Africa. From 1968 to 1971, Walter worked for the Lutheran World Federation as their Consultant on Family Counseling to the churches in Africa. During the 1970s, the Trobisches continued to give marriage seminars in Africa, but marriage guidance was no longer the cutting edge missional concern that it was in the 1960s.

As the Trobisches lost influence in Africa, they shifted their focus to the United States. Just as they had offered Africans various tools to navigate changing sexual norms, so they offered American evangelicals tools to navigate the sexual revolution of the 1960s and 1970s. Chapter 5 discusses the appeal of the Trobisches among American evangelicals and shows how the Trobisches' familiarity with sexuality, gender, and counseling in Africa enabled them to speak into the American situation with refreshing perspective and nuance. Ultimately, the Trobisches played a significant role in shaping a transcultural conversation about the meaning of Christian marriage during the mid-twentieth century.

1

Pioneer Missionaries in Tcholliré, Cameroon

Many missionaries have been drawn to the vocation by evangelical speeches with conscience-rousing rhetoric and catchy slogans, but Walter Trobisch was not one of these. Walter ended up in Africa because he fell in love with Ingrid Joanna Hult, a woman he had met while studying in the United States in 1948 and who had become a missionary teacher in northern Cameroon. The two married in Germany in 1952 and returned to Cameroon a year later. During their first term as pioneer missionaries in the town of Tcholliré, the Trobisches' approach to marriage was deeply entwined with their approach to mission, and both were strongly influenced by nineteenth- and twentieth-century Western gender ideals. It was not until the very end of their three years in Tchollire that the Trobisches began to be able to disentangle Christian teaching from mere Western biases and to begin to appreciate certain aspects of African culture.

"PROOF THAT GOD HAD SOMETHING IN MIND WITH ME"

Walter Trobisch (1923–1979) grew up in Nazi Germany. He was born in Leipzig in 1923, and in 1934, when he was 11, Hitler established one-party rule in Germany. In 1938, Hitler annexed Austria and the Sudetenland, an area of Czechoslovakia inhabited by ethnic Germans.[1] In 1939, wanting to

---

1. Epstein, *Nazi Germany,* 118.

expand German rule even further, Hitler invaded Poland. Britain and France had tolerated his expansion in Austria and Czechoslovakia, but after he invaded Poland they declared war.[2] In 1941, when he was eighteen, Trobisch was drafted into the Nazi army and sent to fight on the Russian front.

Looking back on his experience of the war, Trobisch saw God's hand preserving him. He was wounded in Stalingrad in 1942, right before German troops surrendered to the Russians. Two hundred thousand German troops ended up dying in the battle for Stalingrad, and when Germany surrendered in early 1943, only 5,000 troops made it back to Germany.[3] Trobisch assigned special significance to the fact that he was injured and taken back to Germany just before the Germans were "overrun by the enemy." He decided that this was "proof that God had something in mind with me. His protecting hand became an obligation to give him my whole life."[4]

Trobisch returned to the front and was again wounded in 1943. He was then taken to Vienna to recover. Eager to begin dedicating his life to God, he got permission to study theology at the University of Vienna. While at Vienna, he was "very nearly the only student." Trobisch remembered "times when the professors saw him on the street and exclaimed, 'There goes our student!'"[5]

When Trobisch returned to the front in 1944, he held Bible studies with his fellow soldiers. After the war he decided to continue his study of theology at the University of Leipzig. Leipzig had come under Russian rule. While studying at the university, Trobisch also worked at the ecclesiastical youth office and served as a Protestant representative to "the Leipzig youth council, which included, besides himself, a Catholic and ten Communists."[6] The day he heard that the council had met without him, he suspected he might have done something to offend the authorities. Fearing for his life, he left Leipzig the next morning, intending to find a way across the border into West Germany. "At the border he was befriended by a farmer. He remained for a time, pretending to work in the fields right under the Russian watchtowers. He noticed that every day at noon, the guards left their posts to go into a restaurant."[7] One day he walked across the border while the guards were eating their lunch. Once in West Germany, Trobisch continued his theological education at the University of Heidelberg and Theologische Schule Bethel bei Bielefeld.

2. Epstein, *Nazi Germany*, 123.
3. Epstein, *Nazi Germany*, 184.
4. W. Trobisch to Sudan Mission Committee, 5 July 1951, Ingrid Trobisch Papers.
5. Mattson, "Soldier of the Cross," 7.
6. Trobisch, *On Our Way Rejoicing*, 97.
7. Trobisch, *On Our Way Rejoicing*, 97.

THE TROBISCHES' COURTSHIP

In 1948, Trobisch got a scholarship to study in the United States. He spent two semesters at Augustana Seminary in Rock Island, Illinois, and it was there that he met Ingrid Hult, who had graduated from Augustana College in 1947. When he met her, Hult was in the process of joining the Sudan Mission. Trobisch attended the church service during which Hult was commissioned to be a missionary.

Trobisch returned to Germany in 1949 and eventually became an assistant pastor in Ludwigshafen. Hult moved to France the same year in order to study French for her mission assignment in French-speaking Cameroon. In December of 1949 she received a letter from Trobisch, who had found out from her newsletter that she was in France. Trobisch invited her to come speak at a youth rally, which she did in February of 1950.[8]

As they got to know each other and a romance started to develop, Trobisch showed Hult "an entry he had made in his notebook when he was thirteen. He had written down the reasons for his wanting to become a missionary to Africa."[9] At the time, he had been listening to Bach's "St. Matthew Passion." It was in listening that he suddenly had the overwhelming sense that God was calling him to be a missionary.[10] Interestingly, the Trobisches' son David believes that Walter never did have a "missionary call" comparable to Ingrid's.[11] Ingrid's parents had been missionaries in Tanzania. She had been born in Tanzania, and missionary lore was an integral part of her youth. Four of her ten siblings became missionaries. Even if Walter did hear God call him to mission at the age of thirteen, it was an isolated experience in a childhood otherwise unconcerned with mission. When Walter got a renewed appreciation for his faith during World War II, thoughts of mission do not seem to have entered his head. Rather, he studied theology and expected to pursue ordained ministry in Germany.

It was only through his relationship with Ingrid that Walter began to consider mission as a real career option. He and Ingrid wrote letters to each other during her first year as a missionary in Poli, Cameroon, and their relationship grew.[12] Soon they were engaged. They married in Germany on June 2, 1952, and reflected together on whether they should return to Cameroon. They prayed about this decision, listed the pros and

---

8. Trobisch, *On Our Way Rejoicing*, 92.
9. Trobisch, *On Our Way Rejoicing*, 98.
10. W. Trobisch to Sudan Mission Committee, 5 July 1951, Ingrid Trobisch Papers.
11. D. Trobisch, interview, 4 September 2010.
12. Trobisch, *On Our Way Rejoicing*, 98–109.

cons of returning to Cameroon, and shared their lists with each other.[13] Ultimately, they decided that God was calling them to return, so Walter submitted an application to become a missionary with the Sudan Mission. The Sudan Mission accepted him, but there was still a significant obstacle to surmount. The Trobisches had heard that no German citizen had been allowed in Cameroon since the end of World War I, so when Walter was granted a visa to work in Cameroon, the Trobisches took it as divine confirmation of their plans.[14]

PIONEER MISSIONARIES IN TCHOLLIRÉ

The Trobisches arrived in the port city of Douala, Cameroon on their first wedding anniversary, June 2, 1953.[15] From there, they traveled by rail, truck, and motorcycle eight hundred miles north to Tchollire (pronounced, cho-li-REY), the French capital of the territory of Rey Bouba. The name "Rey Bouba" referred not only to the territory in which the Trobisches would be the first resident missionaries but also to the capital city of the territory.[16]

The Trobisches' mission post in Rey was especially meaningful for Ingrid because her father, Ralph Hult, had been one of the first missionaries to pass through Rey. He had been commissioned to survey Africa for the Augustana Synod, which had decided at their annual convention in 1917 to open up a mission field in Africa.[17] Because of World War I, Hult did not reach Africa until November of 1919. During Hult's survey of the region he met Jamaha, the ruler of Rey. Upon completion of his survey, Hult proposed to the Augustana mission board that they establish a mission site in Rey. However, the board chose instead to send him and his wife Gertrude to Tanganyika. For Ingrid, taking up residence in Rey in order to continue the work her father had envisioned thirty years earlier, was highly satisfying.

In their approach to mission, the Trobisches emulated others in the Sudan Mission. They planted a garden, worked at learning Fulani, and ran a dispensary out of their house. When they arrived in Rey, Jamaha's son Hamada was ruling the region. Aware of the need to maintain good relations with Hamada, the Trobisches made the twenty-five-mile journey from Tchollire

13. Trobisch, *On Our Way Rejoicing*, 116–17.

14. I. Trobisch to friends, May 1953, Ingrid Trobisch Papers. In actuality, there were Germans living in Cameroon at this time (Chiabi, *Making of Modern Cameroon*, 85).

15. Trobisch, *On Our Way Rejoicing*, 119–20.

16. Christiansen, *For the Heart of Africa*, 132–33.

17. The Educational Committee of the Augustana Foreign Missionary Society, *Missionary Calendar*, 51.

to his court as soon as the rainy season had passed and the rivers permitted crossing. When they arrived, Hamada demonstrated an interest in Walter's motorcycle, so Walter showed it off by riding around the inner courtyard.[18] At 6'7", Hamada was an imposing figure for the young missionaries, but they forged ahead with their plan to tell the Christmas story with "colored flannelgraph pictures."[19] According to a letter they sent out to friends in March of 1954, their visit was a success. Hamada seemed to enjoy the story and told them to share it with "all the people of Rey," some 50,000 people.[20]

Whether the Trobisches were at this point unaware of the huge obstacles to Muslim conversion or whether they were simply full of hope and optimism is unclear. In most parts of Africa, "potential Muslim converts faced harsh familial or communal deterrents which typically included abduction, assault and the prospect of losing inheritance, property and child-custody rights."[21] Although Hamada was at first relatively friendly with the missionaries, it would not be long before he changed his mind about them. Ingrid credited Hamada's initial warm welcome in part to the meeting between their fathers thirty years earlier. She wrote in a letter to friends that Hamada seemed touched by the story she told him "about her father's visit with his father in 1921."[22] He was especially struck by the fact that "both fathers died in the same year." It is possible that the family history paved the way for Hamada's openness to the Trobisches. However, judging by Hamada's interest in Walter's motorcycle and the Sudan Mission's plan to open an industrial school in Tchollire, it seems more likely that Hamada welcomed the Trobisches primarily for their ability to connect him with medicine and technology.[23] During the Trobisches' visit, Hamada probed their medical and technological knowledge, asking questions such as: "Are you able to see what is wrong when a person is sick? . . . Why are the white children much stronger than the native children?"[24]

Although the Trobisches felt genuinely optimistic about Hamada's openness to the gospel message, they also recognized that their "point of contact" had to be "along practical lines."[25] Thus on their next visit to Rey,

---

18. "News from Tchollire," no date (likely from Fall of 1953), Ingrid Trobisch Papers.

19. W. and I. Trobisch to friends, March 1954, Ingrid Trobisch Papers.

20. W. and I. Trobisch to friends, March 1954, Ingrid Trobisch Papers.

21. Sharkey, "Missionary Legacies," 68.

22. "News from Tchollire," no date (likely from Fall of 1953), Ingrid Trobisch Papers.

23. An industrial school is a school that teaches students some form of trade or industry.

24. "News from Tchollire," no date (likely from Fall of 1953), Ingrid Trobisch Papers.

25. "News from Tchollire," no date (likely from Fall of 1953), Ingrid Trobisch Papers.

they went with their medicine box. The residents of Rey were eager for the medicine they offered, and Hamada himself requested a shot of penicillin for his mother.[26] In 1955, when they took a missionary nurse with them on a visit to Rey, she "treated 250 patients in 3 days."[27]

In addition to their medical outreach to the community, the Trobisches also began a small school in their home.[28] Walter taught the beginners and Ingrid the more advanced, and before they had better materials, they used the wall of their house as a blackboard.[29] Throughout the next year, they held church services, taught baptism classes as people expressed interest in conversion, and made an evangelism trip to visit the Laka people, one hundred miles west of Tchollire.[30]

MARRIAGE AND GENDER ROLES IN TCHOLLIRÉ

The Trobisches' first years as missionaries in Tchollire were also their first years of married life. Consequently, they were learning what it meant to be missionaries at the same time as they were learning what it meant to be husband and wife. Ingrid believed that their isolation from friends and family was, in fact, a favorable environment in which a newly married couple could grow. She and Walter learned to express their needs and to meet the needs of the other. They learned to accommodate and to forgive.

Walter and Ingrid had a similar commitment to their Christian faith, but in other respects they were incredibly different people. Ingrid was patient, sensitive, and affirming of others.[31] Walter's personality was more intense. He was fond of jokes but also prone to melancholy.[32] The two also came from wildly different backgrounds. Walter grew up in Leipzig, one of the most cultured cities in Europe. His parents were teachers; he had one sister, who died during World War II, and one brother. He loved opera, read the German classics, and retained his appreciation of good literature throughout his life. Ingrid was born to missionary parents in Moshi, Tanzania. She and her nine brothers and sisters spent their youth in the Missouri Ozarks. Ingrid's favorite place was against the trunk of an old

---

26. W. and I. Trobisch to friends, October 1954, Ingrid Trobisch Papers.
27. W. and I. Trobisch to friends, May 15, 1955, Ingrid Trobisch Papers.
28. Trobisch, *On Our Way Rejoicing*, 136.
29. I. Trobisch, Interview by Robert Shuster
30. W. and I. Trobisch to friends, March 1954, Ingrid Trobisch Papers.
31. H. Heil, email, 22 November 2011.
32. H. Heil, email, 22 November 2011.

maple tree, where she could find peace and quiet.[33] Entertainment for the Hult family was the singing of Lutheran hymns and the telling of stories from their parents' missionary travels.

In her journals and later in her published books, Ingrid would write about how Walter was not the type of man she expected herself to marry, but their marriage was one that she believed God had ordained.[34] In spite of their belief that God approved of their marriage, the Trobisches' divergent backgrounds and personalities contributed particular challenges over the course of their marriage. For example, Walter never understood why Ingrid could not just sit and appreciate the beauty of a Wagner opera but insisted on doing needlework or some other task while she was listening.[35] Ingrid was often frustrated that Walter could not or would not express his emotions.[36] Walter spoke German to Ingrid, and she spoke English to him.[37] No doubt the Trobisches' early years of marriage were frustrating at times, but sharing life stories and getting to know one another also kindled the Trobisches' love and appreciation of each other.

Besides simply sharing more of their life stories with one another, the Trobisches also came up with other strategies for coping with the loneliness and isolation of life in Tchollire. For example, they reserved Friday night as "game night." They wound up their record player, played one of the three records they owned, and created space for relaxation and enjoyment. The mail typically came on Fridays, so this added to the joy of the evening.[38] They also made sure their home was a place where they could feel comfortable and refreshed after the challenges of the day. As Ingrid wrote in her autobiography, "Walter and I found it important to have a neat and tastefully furnished home in which we could relax after . . . exhausting mornings. Our two rooms, with the beautiful picture on the wall, the fresh vase of flowers, and even the brightly decorated table, helped to restore us after the heart-rending sight of human suffering."[39]

In their efforts to cultivate marital intimacy and keep a neat and orderly home, the Trobisches were doing what generations of missionary couples in rural Africa had done before them. For example, nineteenth-century missionaries Adolphe and Adèle Mabille retired to their room every day

33. Youngdale, *On My Way Home*, 17.
34. Youngdale, *On My Way Home*, 65.
35. D. Trobisch, interview, 4 September 2010.
36. Nyquist, email, 20 December 2010.
37. D. Trobisch, interview, 4 September 2010.
38. I. Trobisch, Interview by Robert Shuster.
39. Youngdale, *On My Way Home*, 137.

after lunch in order to pray for their children, friends, and workers.[40] And François and Christina Coillard made sure to take time each day for rest and refreshment. "Even during our long explorations . . . we always had the table laid properly once a day at least, and paid each other the compliment of smartening ourselves up," François said.[41]

Historian Dana Robert has observed that missionary attention to cultivating an exemplary marriage and home life is itself a distinct missionary strategy. This missiology of the Christian home, she argues, has been a "cornerstone of Anglo-American missionary thought and practice."[42] In the words of American Board Secretary Rufus Anderson, "The heathen should have an opportunity of seeing Christian families."[43] Sending married couples to the field became a hallmark of evangelical Protestant mission.

Couples developed various ways of handling the division of labor that came with married life on the mission field. Some couples worked alongside each other, translating the Bible into the local language and traversing the countryside to evangelize.[44] Other couples maintained the gender roles that were popular in their home countries, whereby men occupied the public sphere and women, the private sphere. Among these couples, some found the Victorian gender roles completely acceptable. Although they faced struggles peculiar to their role—the husband as an itinerant evangelist, away for months at a time, the wife, caring for children at home—each viewed the sacrifices as part of his/her missionary commitment.[45] Other couples that held to Victorian gender roles on the mission field found them oppressive.[46]

For their part, Walter and Ingrid did not operate under strictly divided gender roles in their early mission career. While they did some gender specific work, such as Walter's preaching and Ingrid's attending at births, they shared most of the duties of their mission life. They both taught, handed out medical supplies from their dispensary, and went on evangelism trips to the surrounding area. Part of the reason for this was that they were the only missionaries in Tchollire. Had they been at a larger mission station they might have had more gender-segregated work.

---

40. Smith, *Mabilles of Basutoland*, 234.
41. Mathews, *Dauntless Women*, 36.
42. Robert, "'Christian Home,'" 134.
43. Anderson, "Introductory Essay," xi.
44. Dana Robert calls Ann Judson an example of this "activistic" type of missionary wife (Robert, *American Women in Mission*, 45).
45. Robert and Mary Moffat are an example of this type of missionary couple (Moffat, *Lives of Robert and Mary Moffat*, 304).
46. Grimshaw, *Paths of Duty*; Hunter, *Gospel of Gentility*.

Because they shared so many of their missionary duties, the Trobisches developed a highly satisfying sense of marital partnership. This was enhanced by the fact that they lacked access to the relational, material, and spiritual resources that were available to their peers in Europe and America. They had no church community, no family or friends in the region, and few material possessions. They simply had to depend on one another to a greater degree than their peers back home. The Trobisches' partnership also grew from the fact that they adhered to the same value system. Barbara Epstein has pointed out that during the nineteenth-century, couples in the United States began to operate under opposing value systems. "In order to succeed in the new world of commercial capitalism, men had to learn to separate morality and sentiment from self-interest, while women, in legitimizing their own domestic activity, called upon the values of the society that commercial capitalism was engaged in destroying."[47] When the Trobisches began their work in Tchollíré in 1953, most of their peers in Europe and America were living in separate spheres under opposing value systems. The Trobisches, and missionaries like them, did not see a sharp dichotomy between the private and the public, between home and work. One result of this was that nineteenth- and twentieth-century missionary wives were far more "incorporated" into the work of their husbands than other Western women in the nineteenth and twentieth centuries.[48]

Being equal partners in mission and in marriage made Walter and Ingrid immune to much of the cultural ferment that was building in the West. Since the early nineteenth century, the identity of middle- and upper-class women in the West had been shifting from producer to consumer. "This loss of function, and of self-esteem that went with it," led ultimately to the feminist movement of the 1960s and 1970s.[49] While their peers in the West were beginning to debate the relative merits of life in the home versus life in the public sector, mission life allowed both Walter and Ingrid to participate in the public and private sphere and to derive a sense of purpose from each. Ingrid was quite right to compare their life to that of her pioneer ancestors in Nebraska: "Our life here has all the aspects of good old pioneer life and I think often of our forefathers as they settled out in western Nebraska and the parallel of life here."[50] In their ability to pursue a common goal, follow the same value system, and avoid a strict dichotomy between the private and

---

47. Epstein, *Politics of Domesticity*, 62.

48. Kirkwood, "Protestant Missionary Women," 40. Her reference to "incorporation" comes from Callan and Ardener, *Incorporated Wife*.

49. Harris, *Beyond Her Sphere*, 56–57.

50. "News from Tchollíré," no date (likely from Fall of 1953), Ingrid Trobisch Papers.

public spheres, the Trobisches lived in Tcholliré in the manner of Ingrid's pioneer ancestors. And that pioneer life was, in some ways, more satisfying than life in 1950s America.

CHANGES IN TCHOLLIRÉ

Although the Trobisches shared nearly all the early tasks of mission life in Tcholliré, their different personalities and skills began to draw them into more specialized work. Of the two, Walter was the intellectual, and the Sudan Mission capitalized on this right away. In January of 1954, Walter was asked to deliver a series of talks at the annual conference. He chose to speak on what he called soul-counseling (in German, *Seelsorge*).[51] Soul-counseling, he argued, should be at the heart of all Christian mission. It is the process whereby one person hears a word from God and delivers it humbly but assuredly to another person. Soul-counseling, he argued further, is not only a necessary skill for Christians on the mission field but for all Christians.

Trobisch urged his colleagues to be bold in their soul-counseling. "What is lacking today," he said, "is aggressive soul-counselling."[52] He told his colleagues that people did not always recognize their need for it. Thus it was imperative that each person occasionally approach a colleague with an invitation for counseling. Making sure to practice what he preached, he said that he was thankful when someone at the conference approached *him* in order to give him space to talk about his problems. His talks must have been well received because the Trobisches included excerpts from them in their station letters of 1954. And Trobisch was asked to lead a series of Bible studies at the next annual conference.[53]

After the annual conference of 1954, André Garba and Paul Darman came with their families to live with the Trobisches in Tchollire.[54] The two men had become Christians through the work of the Sudan Mission in the south. They aspired to be pastors and eventually became the first African pastors in the Sudan Mission. Since the Sudan Mission did not yet have a seminary, the Trobisches agreed to give Garba and Darman pre-seminary training in French, Old and New Testament, exegesis, hermeneutics, and homiletics.[55]

---

51. W. and I. Trobisch to friends, 1 May 1954, Walter Trobisch Collection, Box 12.
52. W. and I. Trobisch to friends, 1 June 1954, Walter Trobisch Collection, Box 12.
53. W. and I. Trobisch to friends, 10 December 1954, Walter Trobisch Collection, Box 12.
54. Trobisch, *On Our Way Rejoicing*, 147.
55. W. and I. Trobisch to friends, 1 June 1954, Walter Trobisch Collection, Box 12.

In addition to studying with the Trobisches, Garba and Darman also assisted the Trobisches in teaching the baptism classes and evangelizing the surrounding area. Their presence in Tcholliré with their families, their decision to sacrifice the familiarity and kinship networks of home, increased what Ingrid called "the effectiveness of our witness."[56] The men's ability to understand African customs and communicate more easily than the Trobisches contributed to the growth of the church in Rey. By the spring of 1954, over twenty people were coming to the baptism classes in Tcholliré. The Trobisches' relationship with Hamada continued to develop favorably with successive visits. Walter, together with Garba, Darman, and fifteen catechumens, developed a play based on the biblical story of the Prodigal Son (Luke 15:11–32), which they performed on evangelistic trips to the east and to the south.[57] By Christmas of 1954, the Trobisches baptized the first Christian converts in Tcholliré.[58]

The year 1955 brought some of the first major opposition to the Trobisches and the young church in Tcholliré. Firstly, the progress of several of the Trobisches' catechumens and converts was impeded in various ways. One was "called back to her home village by her relatives," one decided to take "a second wife as revenge for the unfaithfulness of his first wife," and a few were summoned by Hamada to work in other parts of Rey.[59] Secondly, Hamada forbade the Trobisches from making any evangelistic trips without first acquiring his permission. The Trobisches noted in their letter to friends in 1955, "This does not yet mean that he prohibits our evangelistic activity, but evidently he wants to watch it closely."[60] In the years to come, Hamada's opposition to Christianity would grow. By 1967, he would encourage Muslims in Rey to burn chapels throughout the area, imprison Christians, and construct mosques.[61] In 1955, however, he was not yet hostile to the missionaries or to African Christians.

Despite the obstacles of 1955, the year also brought the Trobisches encouragement and hope. Two new missionaries, Ernest and Helen Johnson, arrived to run the industrial school. While the Trobisches had learned strategies for dealing with their feelings of isolation during their first year in Tcholliré, the arrival of the Johnsons reenergized them for the work at

---

56. W. and I. Trobisch to friends, 1 May 1954, Walter Trobisch Collection, Box 12.

57. W. and I. Trobisch to friends, 11 October 1954, Walter Trobisch Collection, Box 12.

58. W. and I. Trobisch to friends, 15 May 1955, Walter Trobisch Collection, Box 12.

59. W. and I. Trobisch to friends, Fall 1955, Ingrid Trobisch Papers.

60. W. and I. Trobisch to friends, Fall 1955, Ingrid Trobisch Papers.

61. Nygard, "Preaching in Rey Bouba," 17.

hand and increased their sense of both spiritual and physical camaraderie. The four gathered every morning for prayer and reflection and followed the same routine that the Trobisches had established for themselves. Adapting a practice that the reformer Martin Luther had developed, they asked themselves four questions: (1) What do I have to be thankful for? (2) What do I have to pray for? (3) What am I sorry for? and (4) What is my next step?[62] The Johnsons also helped with the baptism and discipleship classes. From the Trobisches' perspective, the Johnsons had come just in time, for "the four of us are scarcely enough to teach all those who come daily to school for Biblical instruction and on Sundays our chapel will soon be too small."[63]

FAMILY LIFE EDUCATION, "AN OPEN DOOR FOR MISSIONS"

On August 22, 1955, Ingrid gave birth to their first child, Katrine Herta. Like many missionary mothers before her, Ingrid found that the women of Tcholliré opened up to her in a new way after she became a mother.[64] The women observed with interest the way little Katrine grew healthy and strong. They also saw how Walter shared the duties of carrying the child. The women then questioned Ingrid about these things. Walter's favorite response, when accused of being unmanly by carrying a child, was to note gaily, "Before the baby was born madam carried the baby, now monsieur can carry it."[65] Both he and Ingrid were pleased to see when some of the men in the village decided that they, too, could carry around their little ones.

As soon as Walter and Ingrid discovered that Walter carrying baby Katrine was a lesson on marital partnership for their observing neighbors, they made a point of having Walter carry the baby often. This process, by which unintentional actions become infused with missiological significance, has a long and fruitful history. Dana Robert has noted that making daily life into "object lessons" has been a classic strategy for missionary wives.[66] In fact, it has given missionary wives a deeper sense of integration between their domestic and mission work.

Prior to having a child of her own, Ingrid's advice was often disregarded when she assisted with births in Tcholliré. On one occasion, a woman pregnant with her first child went into labor and was refused food and water. Ingrid

---

62. W. and I. Trobisch to friends, 15 May 1955, Ingrid Trobisch Papers.
63. W. and I. Trobisch to friends, Fall 1955, Walter Trobisch Collection, Box 12.
64. Trobisch, *On Our Way Rejoicing*, 160.
65. I. Trobisch, Interview by Robert Shuster.
66. Robert, *American Women in Mission*, 65.

tried to recommend sustenance, but to no avail. "All our objections were in vain," wrote Ingrid to friends later.[67] "Because the labor lasted unusually long, the woman finally died from exhaustion." After Ingrid became a mother, she found that her advice gradually gained a hearing among the other mothers in the village, and she and Helen Johnson, who was a nurse, began leading classes in prenatal care, nutrition, and childcare.[68]

Around this time, one of the men who was baptized the previous Christmas took a second wife. Perplexed, Walter asked the man, "Don't you love your wife?" The man told Walter that he took a second wife precisely *because* he loved his first wife. She was pregnant with their first child, and since couples were to abstain from sexual relations until the child was two or three years old, he took a second wife. The Trobisches learned that in many traditional African societies, women tended to abstain from sex during pregnancy and lactation, lest the semen poison the child.[69] The man knew Western Christians opposed polygamy, but he claimed to have taken a second wife out of concern for his wife and the child in her womb. The Trobisches concluded that one way to make polygamy less culturally necessary would be to show that it was not possible for semen to come into contact with a developing fetus. Ingrid and Helen began to teach couples everything they knew about reproductive anatomy, the biological cycles of a woman's body, and the process of conception.

Another problem the Trobisches and Johnsons encountered, however, was the fact that couples in Tchollíré used this sexual taboo during pregnancy and lactation to space out the birth of their children. If a mother got pregnant while she was nursing an infant, her milk might be reduced and the newborn child might starve. This is likely why the idea developed that semen could poison a child. In their eagerness to correct mistaken biological knowledge and fight polygamy, it is doubtful that the Trobisches recognized how the sexual taboo during lactation actually protected both the mother and the newborn child.

What the Trobisches did recognize was that in order for monogamy to become a more feasible option, couples would have to be given alternative methods of birth control.[70] The only method of natural family planning available at the time was the rhythm method. The Trobisches began teaching couples that they could abstain from sex during the woman's fertile period

---

67. W. and I. Trobisch to friends, Fall 1955, Walter Trobisch Collection, Box 12.
68. I. Trobisch, Interview by Robert Shuster.
69. Mpolo, "Polygamy in Pastoral Perspectives," 104–5.
70. It is important to note that there were many other reasons behind the practice of polygamy (Mpolo, "Polygamy in Pastoral Perspectives," 101).

in the middle of her monthly cycle, rather than for an entire two years. For couples hoping to become pregnant, the Trobisches urged them to have sex during the fertile period.

The Trobisches were pleased to be offering useful information to couples in Tchollliré, but neither they nor the people in Tchollliré were satisfied with the rhythm method. Due to the irregularity of women's cycles, the rhythm method was not completely effective, either for avoiding or achieving pregnancy. Thus began the Trobisches' search for a more effective method. They began to pay attention to the latest research on human fertility and natural family planning. They wanted a method "which met the following conditions: (a) it had to be reliable; (b) it should be inexpensive; (c) the application should not involve any health risks; (d) no doctor's help or supervision should be necessary; (e) it should be applicable and accessible for every couple, even in the remote African bush."[71] It would not be until the 1970s that the Trobisches would find such a method (the symptothermal method) and Ingrid would popularize it with her 1975 book *The Joy of Being a Woman*.

For both Walter and Ingrid, correcting misconceptions about fertility, conception, and childbirth became what they would later call "an open door for missions."[72] Children were an integral part of African society and were, in many ways, the glue that held husband and wife together.[73] Theologian John Mbiti wrote in his book *Love and Marriage in Africa*:

> In some African societies, marriage is not fully recognized or consummated until the wife has given birth. First pregnancy becomes, therefore, the final seal of marriage, the sign of complete integration of the woman into her husband's family and kinship circle. Unhappy is the woman who fails to get children. . . . [H]er failure to bear children is worse than committing genocide; she has become the dead end of human life, not only for the genealogical line but also for herself. . . . She will suffer for this, her own relatives will suffer for this; and it will be an irreparable humiliation for which there is no source of comfort in traditional life.[74]

Couples in Tchollliré who struggled to get pregnant welcomed the fertility information the Trobisches delivered. It functioned as a "point of contact," just as the medicine box, Walter's motorcycle, and the industrial

71. Trobisch, *Joy of Being a Woman*, 42.
72. Trobisch, *My Journey Homeward*, 63.
73. Oheneba-Sakyi and Takyi, "Introduction to the Study of African Families," 12.
74. Mbiti, *African Religions and Philosophy*, 110–11.

school had functioned as "points of contact" with Hamada two years earlier. And the Trobisches viewed fertility information with the same level of optimism that they had earlier viewed medicine and technology. They hoped the interest in fertility information would lead to interest in Christian faith.

However, conversion was not the Trobisches' sole aim in disseminating fertility information. They also believed that helping couples manage their fertility was a way of serving God. Genesis 2:24 called for husband and wife to "cleave" or "be united" together.[75] Even if the couples they interacted with never converted to Christianity, the Trobisches believed that by helping couples to "cleave," they were doing something that was pleasing to God. Teaching couples about natural family planning enhanced their ability to either achieve or avoid pregnancy, and this strengthened marriages. Fertility awareness allowed couples to resume sexual relations much sooner than the traditional two years, and this, the Trobisches believed, also served to enhance marital satisfaction.

During their own courtship and early years of marriage, the Trobisches were guided in their understanding of marriage by Swiss physician and marriage counselor Theodor Bovet. Bovet was both their "counselor and trusted friend."[76] He taught that "love should govern the whole field of sexuality, and . . . God should govern the whole field of love."[77] This was the heart of the argument he sought to make in his books and in his personal counseling with individual couples like the Trobisches. During the 1950s one of the most popular conceptions of marriage in German Lutheran circles was that marriage was a way of enacting the divine order of creation. Because God made man before he made woman, man was to rule over woman in the church, in society, and in marriage. Bovet's understanding of marriage was in some ways compatible with this view, for he believed, "Within the family group each member plays a distinctive part . . . In this sense a sacred order—a 'hierarchy'—governs the family: the husband is its 'head,' the wife its 'heart.'"[78] However, Bovet's understanding of marriage was also incompatible with the understanding of marriage as a hierarchical divine order of creation because Bovet emphasized the idea that marriage was a companionship. "Marriage is an absolute companionship, not only of husband and wife as they are today but of their whole past and future, and

---

75. "Therefore shall a man leave his father and his mother, and shall cleave unto his wife: and they shall be one flesh" (KJV).

76. Youngdale, *On My Way Home*, 87.

77. Bovet, *Love, Skill and Mystery*, xiii.

78. Bovet, *Love, Skill and Mystery*, 128.

not only of husband and wife alone but as they exist before God."[79] It was this idea and the idea that "love should govern the whole field of sexuality" that Bovet stressed over the notion of marriage as hierarchy.

As they talked with couples in Tcholliré about natural family planning and developed their own ideas on marital partnership, the Trobisches were more deeply influenced by Bovet's teaching than by the idea of marriage as a divine order of creation and a hierarchical relationship between husband and wife. Their preference for the companionship view of marriage over the hierarchical view was reinforced by their observations of the division of labor in Tcholliré.

The Trobisches believed that the division of labor in Tcholliré was unjust, leaving women "completely overburdened:"

> From 6 a.m. to 3 p.m. they [women] weeded their gardens, sometimes with a baby on their back. Then they had to fetch wood and water, take care of the children, prepare the food, which included pounding the grain, grinding and sifting it, a process that takes two hours time. Meanwhile the husband was already waiting impatiently for his evening meal, after which he demanded sexual union, in some cases even repeatedly. No wonder that those women often urged their husbands to take second and third wives. They looked at polygamy as a possibility to take once in a while a 'vacation from marriage.'[80]

The Trobisches believed traditional, African gender roles prevented women from enjoying marriage. They noticed that men seemed to love their siblings more than their wives. Later, an African pastor would explain to them that in traditional African society, "a man's wife is like an ambassador from a foreign tribe. He never trusts her like he does his blood brothers and sisters."[81]

The Trobisches began to feel that putting their own marriage on display was the best way of proclaiming the gospel.[82] If their neighbors saw them loving and trusting each other, perhaps their neighbors might better understand how to love and trust Jesus. The Trobisches had found that people had difficulty believing in Jesus as a loving person. They wondered if this was because love was usually reserved for blood relations. Ingrid said, "The fact that Walter and I could live together in love and harmony in our

---

79. Bovet, *Love, Skill and Mystery*, 27–28.

80. W. Trobisch, "The Discrimination of Women," Walter Trobisch Collection, Box 12, Folder 39.

81. I. Trobisch, Interview by Robert Shuster.

82. This is a classic strategy in the history of Christian mission (Robert, "'Christian Home,'" 153–54).

family was perhaps the first way that they could believe [in Jesus]."[83] Just as natural family planning had proven to be a relevant topic, the Trobisches believed that discussing the division of labor and putting their own marriage on display would be "an open door for missions" and a way to improve marital relationships in Tchollíré.

THE TROBISCHES' SHIFTING PERSPECTIVE ON CULTURE, POLITICS, AND MISSION

A Postcolonial Critique of the Trobisches' Perspective on African Women

Like most missionaries of their day, the Trobisches' initial assessment of African culture was negative. Their observation of the division of labor in Tchollíré led them to believe that African culture promoted lazy, demanding men and overburdened, cynical women. This observation, however, was based more on the Trobisches' own conceptions of proper gender relations than on the actual testimonies of African couples themselves. When Trobisch surmised that African women were "completely overburdened" and African men were demanding, he was not making reference to conversations he had had with individual African couples in Tchollíré. Rather, he was interpreting spousal relations in Tchollíré through the lens of Theodor Bovet's theology of marriage, which was written with mid-twentieth-century Europeans in mind.

Throughout the Trobisches' years in Africa, they maintained that they were arguing for a "Christian" view of marriage, but in reality their view of marriage was strongly marked by Western biases and could not therefore be called simply "Christian." Their stress on the partnership of husband and wife was as much a product of changes in the economic structure of Western society as it was a commentary on Genesis 2:24. And yet, the Trobisches preferred to attribute their vision of marital partnership to the Bible and not to Western cultural and economic developments.

Postcolonial scholars have argued that Western feminist discourse tends to "silence the 'native woman' in its pious attempts to represent or speak for her."[84] Similarly, there is a way in which the Trobisches silenced the women of Tchollíré by speaking for them. In their sympathy for African women and in their efforts to free them by teaching a new vision of marriage, the Trobisches were essentially saying that they knew what was best

83. I. Trobisch, Interview by Robert Shuster.
84. Gandhi, *Postcolonial Theory*, 89.

for these women. And as postcolonial critics have so effectively pointed out, this has been the classic stance of the colonialist oppressor. The Trobisches were also blind to some of the ways in which the traditional life may have appealed to African women. For example, Cheryl Johnson-Odim has pointed out that some women in traditional African cultures have "derived a certain autonomy and status from their roles as cultivators, traders, artisans, and providers of other marketplace services."[85]

However, the Trobisches were not alone in thinking that the division of labor and the present state of marriage in Africa discriminated against women. During the 1950s, hundreds of African women began to demand custody rights and to pressure governments to oppose polygamy and reform the bride-price.[86] Women put together charters that stated "woman is equal to man by nature" and should be "as free as man to fulfill her personal destiny and to choose her state of life."[87] Again, Johnson-Odim's perspective is helpful. She notes that even though women in traditional African cultures had ways of gaining autonomy and status, they were also expected to submit to their husbands and parents. In other words, these women were "far more subordinated to men privately than publicly."[88] Furthermore, a married woman often found herself in the awkward position of having to ask her husband to take a second wife even though she didn't want to. As theologian Anne Nasimiyu-Wasike explains, women were expected "to make men wealthy by bearing many children and producing great amounts of food. When a woman found herself unable to cultivate, plant, weed, and harvest enough food due to physical weakness and not having enough children to help her, she was forced to request her husband to bring another or more subordinates."[89] Far from approving of polygamy, women were forced into it because of gender norms and expectations.

The solution proposed by African women theologians in the 1980s and 1990s was not a simple substitution of Western gender ideals for African ones. As Mercy Amba Oduyoye pointed out, the oppression of women in traditional African culture was often not ameliorated but only "strengthened by Western patriarchal structures."[90] Oduyoye's suggestion for how to promote women's flourishing was to ensure that women had equal

---

85. Johnson-Odim, "Actions Louder Than Words," 79.
86. Marie André du Sacré Cœur, *House Stands Firm*, 229–31.
87. Marie André du Sacré Cœur, *House Stands Firm*, 230.
88. Johnson-Odim, "Actions Louder Than Words," 79.
89. Nasimiyu-Wasike, "Polygamy," 111.
90. Oduyoye, *Daughters of Anowa*, 151.

representation in government. She and others also worked tirelessly to combat patriarchy in the church.

Ingrid Trobisch's Growing Respect for African Women

Like Oduyoye, the Trobisches would in later years notice and oppose patriarchy in the church. However, in the late 1950s they could only see how Christianity liberated women. This bias made it difficult for them to see any of the good in traditional African gender norms. However, the more they observed and thought about spousal relations in Tchollire, the more they began to see some of the good in African culture and to develop a more critical perspective on Western culture.

Before she had come to Africa, Ingrid's primary vision of Africans was as "innumerable tribes of heathen . . . despairing in the efficacy of their own religions, [and] stretching out their hands to an unknown God."[91] Although Ingrid would never waver in her desire to evangelize in Africa, her respect for aspects of African culture grew. She began to appreciate the strength, gracefulness, and optimism of the women in Tchollire. They had what she called a "we can do it" attitude. She learned the wisdom behind the African belief that "a lady does not hurry."[92] Ingrid found herself observing with interest the way African mothers gave birth without the aid of anesthesia and nursed their children until the age of two.[93] By comparison, laboring women in the United States in the 1950s often took drugs to reduce the pain of childbirth and opted to give their babies formula instead of breastfeeding.

These observations about the differences between African and American experiences of childbirth and nursing continued to germinate in Ingrid throughout her years in Africa and then in Austria. As she became aware of the various childbirth and nursing movements that were underway in the West, such as Dr. Lamaze's natural childbirth teachings, which he began to publicize in 1951, and the La Leche League (founded in 1956), Ingrid became a vocal participant in these movements. Her desire to make evangelical Christians aware of the natural childbirth and nursing resources available to them eventually culminated in the 1975 publication of her book *The Joy of Being a Woman*.[94]

---

91. Sudan United Mission, "Land of the Blacks: Christ or Mohammed? A Worldwide Warning" (missionary pamphlet for the Sudan Mission), Ingrid Trobisch Papers.

92. I. Trobisch, Interview by Robert Shuster.

93. D. Trobisch, interview, 4 September 2010.

94. See discussion of Ingrid Trobisch's promotion of natural childbirth and breastfeeding in chapter 5, p. 112–16.

Walter Trobisch's Critique of Western Culture

Like Ingrid, although Walter was initially critical of African culture, his experience in Tcholliré also enabled him to develop a critique of Western culture. He began to draw attention to what he called "white" sins, which he defined as "our virtues prefaced by the little word 'too.'"

> Isn't this a picture of an ideal missionary—one who is economical, orderly, generous, diligent, patient, tactful and time-conscious? But if we are too economical, we become stingy; if we are too orderly we become fussy and lost in details; if we are too diligent we become over-worked (this is no merit, but a white sin); if we are too patient we become lenient; if we are too tactful, we become cowardly; if we are too time-conscious, we become nervous.[95]

During their furlough in 1956 and 1957, Trobisch further developed his critique of Western culture. He rebuked American Christians for failing to cultivate true "Christian homes": "Most of our Christian homes are just motels, where you gas up, get some food and sleep, and then go again." A home, he said, should be a place of "quietness and restfulness," where the family and guests can find comfort and nourishment for their soul and body.[96] He argued, "It is sinful to spend more than two evenings a week away from your family," and "your television set does not belong in your living room, where you are supposed to receive and meet people." Trobisch felt that Western Christians neglected nourishing their souls. With typical humor, he remarked in one sermon, "I am impressed how conscientiously the people of Minneapolis take care of their lawns. But sometimes I think, if they would give only half as much care to their souls as they give to their lawns, what could happen!"[97]

Trobisch's ability to critique his own culture was relatively unique among missionaries of his era and grew, in part, from his first-hand experience of war and his time as a student in America. When Trobisch came to the United States as one of the first German, foreign exchange students after World War II, he was repulsed by the happy-go-lucky attitude in American churches.[98] His experience with suffering during the war, with being near death several times, had led him to a deep appreciation of the theology of the cross, the notion that Christ has suffered everything humans suffer and

---

95. W. and I. Trobisch to friends, 21 July 1954, Walter Trobisch Collection, Box 12.
96. Trobisch, "This Was Not Done in a Corner," 7.
97. Trobisch, "This Was Not Done in a Corner," 6.
98. S. Trobisch, interview, 5 September 2010.

can therefore offer comfort to the suffering. Trobisch believed the American churches needed "more preaching that presents the great evangelical message of Christianity that centers around the Cross."[99]

Trobisch was especially disgusted with the entertaining character of so much of the church youth work. In the years to come, Trobisch would continue to see his task in the United States as one of urging the American church to overcome its happy-go-lucky approach to faith. When he spoke in churches in 1957, he deliberately countered the triumphalistic style of typical missionary reports. Instead, he told the congregation, "I have not reported to you a series of victories. By intention, I have not given you an old style report with stories of conversions and Christian happy-end narratives. Instead I have given you a very sober description of the situation as it is."[100]

Part of the sober situation, which Trobisch reported in 1957, was the problem of racism in America. American racism, he declared pointedly, "may result in the loss of the African continent for Christ."[101] He told of an African man who confronted him on a train ride with the question, "Are those whites in the southern states of North America who stand against racial integration Christians?" The man's disgust, said Trobisch, was clear. And so was his conclusion: "Therefore Christianity has no message for us."[102]

Trobisch told another story about Kwame Nkrumah, the first Prime Minister of Ghana, who had studied in America during his student days. On one occasion, when he sought a glass of water from a restaurant, the waiter sent him to the spittoon outside. Nkrumah declared in his autobiography, "I was so shocked that I could not move. I just stood and stared at him for I could not bring myself to believe that anyone could refuse a man a drink of water, because his skin happened to be a different colour."[103] Trobisch told mission sympathizers, "There are still missionaries in Africa who receive the Africans on the back porch, who do not offer them a chair, but have them sit on the floor. . . . Missionaries like that do more damage than good. So if you are not ready to eat with an African at the same table, to share in case of necessity your guest room or even your bedroom with him, you better stay home."[104]

The Trobisches took concrete actions to combat racism in their personal lives. In March of 1956, the Sudan Mission asked them to leave their

99. Mattson, "Soldier of the Cross," 7.
100. Trobisch, "Africa of Tomorrow," 13.
101. Trobisch, "This Was Not Done in a Corner," 5.
102. Trobisch, "Africa of Tomorrow," 1–2.
103. Quoted in Trobisch, "This Was Not Done in a Corner," 4.
104. Trobisch, "This Was Not Done in a Corner," 6.

post in Tcholliré and move to Libamba, southern Cameroon so Walter could teach German at Cameroon Christian College. They remained at Libamba until June, when they left on furlough, and returned to Libamba in time for the start of the 1957 school year. They would live in Libamba until 1963. Throughout their six years there, they worked hard to develop friendships with the African faculty and students in their community. They made sure their children played with all the children on campus, whether African, French, German, Swiss, or American.[105] They asked one of Trobisch's African students to be their son David's godfather. The Trobisches also found that because they were an international couple (Walter was German, Ingrid was American), they "were often asked to help bridge cultural and interpersonal gaps" between people on campus.[106]

Walter Trobisch also worked to raise awareness of the economic impact of Christian mission work. Most of the missionaries the Trobisches knew in Cameroon were unconcerned with the political and economic consequences of their missionary presence. They considered their task to be spiritual in nature and assumed that people who expressed interest in conversion were doing so because they had become aware of their sin and wanted to live a holy life. The Trobisches in no way disagreed with the evangelical goal of bringing people to a place of confession and redemption. However, they grew wary of this naïve, simplistic explanation of conversion.

While on furlough, Walter Trobisch shared his observations about some of the economic factors that contributed to Christian conversion:

> The missionary who comes to Africa today has not only a lantern, kerosene, matches and even a real bed, but also often a car, a radio and a refrigerator. Therefore it is almost unavoidable that the native population gets the impression: you have to become a Christian in order to possess these wonderful things. The Africans are then overcome—not by the power of the Gospel over the world—but by the power of the worldly possessions of the missionary.[107]

Trobisch's observation was echoed by his contemporaries. J. B. Schuyler, observing conversion in Nigeria around the same period, commented, "Christianity has impressed many as being largely a social organization capable of worshipping God and mammon simultaneously, and demanding

---

105. Trobisch and Trobisch, *Adventures of Pumpelhoober,* 26, 41.
106. Youngdale, *On My Way Home,* 99.
107. Trobisch, "Africa of Tomorrow," 1.

payment for the symbols of membership, the administration of the sacraments. Many conversions have been for material reasons."[108]

Trobisch's awareness in 1956 of the intersection between power, race, wealth, and religion in colonial Africa was nowhere near as developed as that of postcolonial theorists of the coming decades. He and Ingrid had only a budding awareness of the way in which their identity as white foreigners in Africa affected their interactions with Africans and affected conversion to their religion. Yet Trobisch wasted no time in sharing this dawning awareness with his supporters and colleagues. He told his supporters that missionary presence in Cameroon helped to create new markets for Western goods, and this was not for God's glory. In fact, it—like racism and inhospitable homes—was something for which missionaries should repent.

The Trobisches' Support of African Nationalism

The movement in Cameroon to gain independence from France was well under way during the Trobisches' first term there. During their three years in Tcholliré, the Trobisches did not give it much thought because it was essentially irrelevant to the lives of the inhabitants of Rey. However, during the three months they spent at Cameroon Christian College prior to leaving on furlough, Walter Trobisch had numerous conversations with students that caused him to become sympathetic to the nationalist cause. In April and May of 1955, the nationalist party (the UPC) held a number of political rallies which were disrupted by anti-UPC groups or by French forces.[109] Between May 22 and 30, several of these incidents turned violent. Each side maintained that the other had initiated the violence.[110] Judging by their letter to friends, the Trobisches thought the UPC had initiated the riots, but they also thought the French had crushed the riots with "unwise and unnecessary harshness."[111] On July 13, 1955, the French government banned the UPC. This decision increased nationalist fervor across Cameroon, the UPC went underground, and civil war began.

Most of the Trobisches' fellow missionaries in Cameroon tried to stay neutral in the nationalist struggle, but Walter Trobisch criticized neutrality as a cowardly stance. He recognized that Western missionaries were in a delicate position. "If we turn against an out-of-date colonialism . . . our attitude is easily interpreted as hostility to the French government and we risk

108. Schuyler, "Conceptions of Christianity," 220.
109. DeLancey et al., *Historical Dictionary*, 7.
110. Joseph, *Radical Nationalism in Cameroun*, 264–88.
111. W. and I. Trobisch to friends, June 1956, Ingrid Trobisch Papers.

the refusal of our visas."[112] Nevertheless, he argued that it was more important for missionaries to support the nationalist movement than to protect their own interests. In a sermon delivered during furlough in America, he said, "It must be stated clearly by us on the mission field as well as by you in the home church: 'Colonialism is sin.'"[113]

The Trobisches' Developing Postcolonial Mission Theory

In addition to supporting African nationalism, the Trobisches also supported postcolonial trends in mission theory. Through sermons given on furlough, Walter Trobisch spoke of the need to abandon the notion of mission as "a one-way street . . . from us to Africa" and to think instead about "a missionary exchange among the Christian churches of the world."[114] He said that many European and American churches would benefit from hearing an African speak from the pulpit, and he challenged the Western congregations, "Would you be humble enough to accept him?"[115]

Trobisch's reference to the end of mission as "a one-way street" was a direct reference to the report of the 1952 meeting of the International Missionary Council in Willingen, Germany.[116] Mission theory at Willingen began to coalesce around a less church-centric view of mission, and in the late 1950s the Trobisches' own perspective of mission was compatible with the developing paradigm. Instead of thinking of mission as proceeding from God to the *Church* to the World, delegates at Willingen argued that mission proceeded from God to the *World* to the Church. With this more world-centric view of mission, it became appropriate to see God's hand at work as much in current events like African nationalism as in the life of the church. Similarly—and this was a point the Trobisches would develop more fully in years to come—it was essential for Christians to address that most worldly of all topics, the topic of human sexuality.

---

112. Trobisch, "Africa of Tomorrow," 6–7.
113. Trobisch, "Africa of Tomorrow, 7.
114. Trobisch, "Africa of Tomorrow," 4.
115. Trobisch, "Africa of Tomorrow," 5.
116. International Missionary Council, *Missionary Obligation*, 4.

2

Composing *J'ai Aimé Une Fille* at Cameroon Christian College in Libamba

Prior to leaving on furlough in the middle of 1956, Walter Trobisch had taught for three months at Cameroon Christian College in Libamba and had grown passionate about the need for Western Christians to support African nationalist movements. When he and Ingrid returned to Cameroon in 1957, they found that in addition to political independence, the students at Libamba also wanted independence in interpersonal relationships. Some wanted to be able to choose their own spouse, rather than having their parents choose for them. Some wanted to abolish the bride-price. Others did not understand why the church would forbid premarital sex. Walter addressed their questions in a little book called *J'ai Aimé Une Fille,* which offered a set of guidelines to help Christians navigate the changes in gender relations in mid-twentieth-century Africa. The book spread rapidly not only in Africa but around the world. It launched the Trobisches into a global marriage counseling ministry.

LIFE AT LIBAMBA DURING THE CAMEROONIAN INDEPENDENCE MOVEMENT

The Cameroonian independence movement was gaining momentum in October of 1957 when the Trobisches returned to the country after a year of furlough. On June 23, 1956, the French National Assembly had passed the *Loi Cadre*, which aimed "to provide an institutional framework for the gradual evolution of overseas territories toward self rule."[1] Nationalist movements in other parts of the French empire (French Indochina, Morocco, Tunisia, and Algeria) and in British West Africa (Ghana, Nigeria) had paved the way for the *Loi Cadre*. Realizing that it could not keep its colonies from developing nationalist sentiments, the French National Assembly passed the *Loi Cadre* as a way of granting just enough independence to its African colonies to avoid the bloody conflict that France had experienced in Indochina and was in the midst of in Algeria.

Cameroonian politicians effectively pressured the French government to do more for Cameroon than what was stipulated in the *Loi Cadre*, and the French National Assembly passed *Statut du Cameroun,* which granted Cameroon control over local affairs (even though Cameroon's military remained under French control).[2] On May 10, 1957, the French appointed Mbida to be the first prime minister in a self-governing Cameroon.

Despite the strides towards independence, however, a civil war had been raging in Cameroon since 1955. The UPC, a radical, nationalistic political party that had been declared illegal in July of 1955, had gone underground at that time and had in December of 1956 turned violent in its opposition to French rule.[3] The Trobisches lived in the midst of insurrection territory. In one of their first letters to friends and supporters, they wrote that the UPC revolutionaries "hid in the huge virgin forest which surrounds us here, raided villages at night, killed and kidnapped people, mostly those who collaborated with the government."[4]

The UPC considered Prime Minister Mbida a French puppet.[5] While the UPC had always advocated immediate independence from France, Mbida held that Cameroon would not be ready for another ten years. In February of 1958, Mbida's government failed and Ahidjo became the prime minister of Cameroon. Ahidjo adopted the two major goals of the UPC: reunification with British Cameroon and immediate independence from France.[6] In some cases, his tactics turned out to be as violent and unethical as those employed by the UPC.

The Trobisches heard reports from people in Libamba that Ahidjo's government was conducting "questionings under application of electric

1. DeLancey et al., *Historical Dictionary*, 232.
2. Le Vine, "Cameroon," 246.
3. Joseph, *Radical Nationalism in Cameroun*, 212, 316.
4. W. and I. Trobisch to friends, April 1958, Ingrid Trobisch Papers.
5. Chiabi, *Making of Modern Cameroon*, 98.
6. DeLancey, *Cameroon*, 40.

current . . . and nightly executions without trial." Eventually, the Trobisches and their colleagues felt that they could "no longer keep silent."[7] The twenty Libamba faculty members, a diverse group of Africans and Europeans, wrote a letter to the UPC and the French government, decrying the unjust actions on both sides and proposing a few solutions. They proposed "an amnesty for all, the reinstatement of the UPC as a legal political party, and the maintenance of a well-controlled police force to prevent acts of personal revenge."[8] Their letter, unsurprisingly, had no discernable effect on either the government or the revolutionaries. However, it allowed the faculty to feel they had at least tried to do something to improve the situation.

By December of 1959, with Cameroon's full political independence only a month away, Walter Trobisch wrote in their family journal, "In the last month the political situation has gotten worse. . . . We have packed our most valuable possessions. . . . In case of danger we could leave in an hour."[9] Ingrid Trobisch had gone by way of plane to the mission hospital at Ngaoundéré to await the birth of their fourth child. Their second child, Daniel Martin, had been born on furlough in Germany on November 5, 1956. And David Johannes had been born in Cameroon on August 18, 1958. Ingrid traveled alone to the hospital in Ngaoundéré, leaving Daniel, David, and their older sister, Katrine, in Libamba with Walter and Walter's mother. Just ten hours after Ingrid's layover in Douala, the UPC revolutionaries attacked the airport there. Walter heard that another attack would occur on January 1, the day of independence, so he advised Ingrid to stay in Ngaoundéré until things settled down. Ingrid gave birth to Stephen Walter on January 25. From back home in Libamba, Walter wrote, "Politically the constructive struggle for independence is changing fast into a destructive tribal warfare."[10] He contacted Ingrid and proposed taking the entire family up to Ngaoundéré to join her, as it was safer there than in Libamba. But by the second week of February, the political situation had stabilized enough for her to come home.

The seven weeks of separation were difficult for the Trobisches. Seven weeks was the longest amount of time they had been apart since being married, and they had to deal with the added stress of an unstable political situation, unreliable mail service, and the uncertainty of when they would next see one another. Moreover, Walter was not enjoying his position as chaplain and professor of German at Libamba. He found it

---

7. W. and I. Trobisch to friends, April 1958, Ingrid Trobisch Papers.
8. W. and I. Trobisch to friends, April 1958, Ingrid Trobisch Papers.
9. W. and I. Trobisch to friends, March 1960, Ingrid Trobisch Papers.
10. W. and I. Trobisch to friends, March 1960, Ingrid Trobisch Papers.

disheartening to spend hours preparing sermons for the college chapel when so many of the students could not even be there, due to the political instability. In desperation, he wrote to Ingrid, "One cannot preach without a congregation—and can a student body ever be a true congregation?"[11] Teaching German was exhausting for him because he had to teach in French and had only a "modest knowledge of French." As they wrote in a letter to friends, "He [Walter] has sometimes to work harder than his students, especially if it comes to translating Goethe and Schiller into French."[12] It was not unusual for Walter to rise before dawn and stay up until midnight to finish his work.[13] As chaplain, Walter also felt that his door should always be open to those who needed counsel. While this open-door policy was important to him, it also meant that he had even less time for his other duties.

The Evangelical Lutheran Church mission board had sent Walter to Libamba to see whether it was the kind of place they would want to duplicate in their own mission efforts. Prior to the Trobisches' furlough, Walter had reported back, "There is no doubt that the importance of this institution will grow, not only for the Camerouns, but also for the whole French-speaking West Africa."[14] Libamba was the only school of its kind in French-speaking West Africa—a Christian College that brought students to the Baccalaureate level on par with the French system. It was founded in 1946 by American and French Presbyterians.[15] Teachers' salaries came from the mission organizations to which the teachers belonged.[16] As "the first and largest Protestant Christian college in French-speaking Africa at that time," Libamba was "the darling" of the PCUSA mission. Students at Libamba took the same exams that were given in France. Because a diploma was their ticket to the best jobs the newly independent country had to offer, the students worked extremely hard at their studies.[17]

However, because Libamba did not have much money, it could not hire all the staff necessary for its functioning. For that reason, the faculty members were required to help out with a number of the general tasks associated with life at a boarding school. The faculty helped in the kitchen and business office, they supervised meals and study periods, led worship, drove

11. W. and I. Trobisch to friends, March 1960, Ingrid Trobisch Papers.
12. W. and I. Trobisch to friends, June 1956, Ingrid Trobisch Papers.
13. W. and I. Trobisch to friends, March 1961, Ingrid Trobisch Papers.
14. W. Trobisch to Dr. Syrdal, 20 July 1956, Ingrid Trobisch Papers.
15. Sunquist and Long, *History of Presbyterian Missions*, 242.
16. Youngdale, *On My Way Home*, 99.
17. W. and I. Trobisch to friends, October 1961, Walter Trobisch Collection, Box 12.

to the post office, and took sick students to the mission hospital. According to David Gelzer, a fellow professor of German at Libamba, Walter Trobisch was particularly bothered by having to help supervise meals. On one occasion, Trobisch exclaimed angrily, "I have important things to do."[18] That he would be required to supervise mealtimes when he had so many more pressing duties—writing sermons, grading papers, counseling students—frustrated him to no end.

Trobisch was also dissatisfied at Libamba because he did not have time to do more creative work, like writing a book. In 1960, Trobisch's frustration had reached a peak; he complained to Ingrid, "This has been one of the hardest weeks of my life."[19] Ingrid tried to comfort him. She pointed out that the work he was doing at Libamba, overseeing the development of his students, was truly godly, creative work. "Just this is the most creative work we shall ever be called to do—far more creative than building a monument, making speeches, or even writing a book! To be partners with God in forming and shaping these 'living stones' is a task humbling and yet the greatest. It's down to earth drudgery and at the same time it opens the door to heaven."[20] Walter was not convinced. And as the years went by he grew more exhausted and frustrated by life at Libamba.

Ingrid Trobisch had her own share of exhaustion from raising their four young children, keeping house, sewing, mending, washing, shopping, gardening, and cooking. Fortunately, she had help from Walter's mother, Gertrude (whom everyone called Mutti). Mutti lived with them from August of 1958 until June of 1961.[21] Hildegard, an African woman who ran a kindergarten at Libamba, also lived with the Trobisches for a number of years. Mutti liked to say that Hildegard was "the oil that keeps things running smoothly," and, as Ingrid wrote in a letter to their friends, "when all four children start screaming at once, we need a little oil to tone things down!"[22] Mutti returned to Germany before the Trobisches' fifth and last child, Ruth Ingrid, was born on September 12, 1961. Hildegard still offered to help Ingrid with the children. Although Ingrid would later testify that the years of having young children were "among the happiest in my life," there were certainly days when she did not feel so cheery and optimistic.[23] Probably her most difficult time came in July of 1962, when Walter went to teach

18. Gelzer, email, 31 August 2010.
19. W. and I. Trobisch to friends, March 1960, Ingrid Trobisch Papers.
20. W. and I. Trobisch to friends, March 1960, Ingrid Trobisch Papers.
21. Trobisch, *On Our Way Rejoicing*, 191–92.
22. Ingrid to Co-Workers, March 1961, Ingrid Trobisch Papers.
23. Youngdale, *On My Way Home*, 108.

a pastors' Refresher Course at Makumira Theological Seminary in Tanzania and was gone for a total of nine weeks.[24] After a month, Ingrid wrote in her journal, "I've been struggling to keep sane and even-tempered surrounded as I am by my five children—Ruth just 10 months up to Kathy not quite seven. Often I've failed miserably and would like to do nothing quite as much as sit down in a desolate corner and weep."[25]

The Trobisches lived in a tin house on stilts, necessary in the damp, humid climate of the primeval forest of southern Cameroon. In the rainy season, it was especially difficult for Ingrid with her five children. Lonely and fed up from being house-bound, due to rain, she wrote, "There are . . . days (today for example) when I wish it would be evening before we even eat breakfast."[26] Mealtimes were the most difficult. Ingrid wrote to Walter, "I just wish you could . . . live through an hour here about supper-time. I don't know whether to scream or laugh when things get too involved with the children. I usually end up doing some of both." Ingrid took comfort on difficult days from the fact that they had been able to have children at all. For four years they had been unable to get pregnant.[27] This gave her perspective and made her grateful for her present life as a mother of five healthy children.

During their three years in Tchollire, the Trobisches had done most of their work side by side. They had had no children, so both of them could be fully engaged with the daily work of evangelizing, teaching, and distributing medicine. Even when they had their first child, it was possible for either Walter or Ingrid to carry baby Katrine around with them wherever they went. Life at Libamba was different. They had two children, Katrine and Daniel, when they arrived in 1957. David was born in 1958, Stephen in 1960, and Ruth in 1961. Having five children in six years took all of Ingrid's energy. She still felt a call to public missionary work, but she had no time to devote to it. At one point she taught a course at Libamba, but in general she had to give up her public mission work in order to raise her children and provide "a haven of rest for my busy husband."[28]

Ingrid knew her work as a mother and housewife was necessary and important, and she would not have traded her five children for the opportunity to be more heavily involved in public mission work at Libamba, but the constant task of subsuming missionary fervor in domestic duties

24. Ingrid to Co-Workers, 8 December 1962, Ingrid Trobisch Papers.
25. I. Trobisch, Journal, 20 July 1962, Ingrid Trobisch Papers.
26. I. Trobisch to Walter and Mutti, 22 July 1962, Ingrid Trobisch Papers.
27. I. Trobisch, Interview by Robert Shuster.
28. Youngdale, *On My Way Home*, 121.

was not easy for her. Generations of missionary mothers have had to go through the same painful process of figuring out how to channel missionary energy into domestic duties.[29]

Had they stayed in Tchollíré rather than moving to Libamba, the Trobisches might have been able to maintain the more equitable division of labor that they had initially established there. They might have been able to work out an arrangement that would have allowed Ingrid to continue to share in the public mission work and Walter to spend more time caring for the children. In her autobiography, Ingrid reflected, "As a German he [Walter] had observed that the care of infants was predominantly the mother's domain, as were kitchen duties and household chores. Yet, he was never one to be trapped into acting a certain way if it didn't make sense."[30] Had they stayed in Tchollíré, it might not have made sense for Ingrid to take over the sole care of home and children. However, in Libamba it did make sense. The children needed care, and Walter's job took so much time that it was not possible for him to be involved in the daily care of the children.

The hectic pace of the Trobisches' life in Libamba and their gender-separate division of labor took a toll on their marriage. Walter spent so much time doing his school work that Ingrid ended up feeling neglected and, according to Walter, worked herself into a "crisis." Ingrid wrote of these episodes in her journal: "Walter's accusation—Every 14 days I make a crisis and forget about all the good things—No wonder he [Walter] gets exasperated. These are tests for me—always when he's absorbed in something else—writing project, soulcare + then I come under this attack."[31] One of the Trobisches' closest friends, Ruth Nyquist, believed Ingrid was especially vulnerable to feelings of neglect because she was a child of missionaries. Such children often feel that their parents are more interested in being missionaries than being parents. According to Nyquist, Ingrid also "admitted to a distant relationship with her mother and she idealized her father who abandoned (my term!) them during WW2."[32] For these reasons, Ingrid tended to expect Walter "to compensate for all her needs," and Walter "found her needs bewildering."[33] Ingrid knew that she needed to learn how to manage her feelings better. In her journal, she wrote that she

29. Robert, *American Women in Mission*, 69; Hunter, *Gospel of Gentility*, 127.
30. Youngdale, *On My Way Home*, 108.
31. I. Trobisch, Journal, 11 June [no year], Ingrid Trobisch Papers.
32. Nyquist, email, 20 December 2010. Ingrid's father left his wife and ten children to go to Africa as a missionary in 1943.
33. Nyquist, email, 20 December 2010.

would try to avoid self-pity, depend on God, and be disciplined. Lastly, she realized that it would be helpful to "have a creative project of my own."[34]

THE BEGINNING OF THE TROBISCHES' WRITING MINISTRY

In 1961, Ingrid Trobisch did embark on a creative project of her own, and it was a project that gave her great joy and helped her feel like she could again fulfill a bit of her public missionary vocation. For a long time, Ingrid had wanted to write the story of her father and his missionary work. In 1961, she wrote to Harper & Row to see if they would be interested in her story. Melvin Arnold, Director of the Religious Department, invited her to send a sample chapter and an outline. Since the only time she had for writing was "an hour after breakfast when the older children were rested, fed, and content while the baby took her morning nap," Walter agreed to watch the children for two hours in the afternoon.[35] After two weeks of writing, Ingrid mailed off her sample chapter and outline. A few weeks later she received a letter from Arnold, offering her a contract and inviting her to come to New York City to discuss the book. Ingrid was ecstatic. Over the course of the next year, she corresponded with Edward Sammis, the contractor Harper & Row had appointed to be her editor, and began working on her book.

Although neither Walter nor Ingrid realized it at the time, Ingrid's book contract marked a turning point in their career. Until this point, the Trobisches fit the stereotypical image of a Western, missionary couple. In 1953, they had moved to a remote village in Africa. In 1957, Walter had taken the teaching post at Libamba and Ingrid had withdrawn from the public mission work in order to take care of their five children. In the history of mission, most missionary mothers have not had time to write a book.[36] Ingrid not only wrote a book, but her book facilitated the Trobisches' transition to a different sort of mission work. In the late 1960s and 1970s, writing, rather than itinerant evangelism or college teaching, became their primary ministry. As Ingrid wrote later in her autobiography, the publication of *On Our Way Rejoicing* in 1964 "was the beginning of our writing ministry, with its ever-widening circles."[37] Ingrid and Walter both

---

34. I. Trobisch, Journal, 11 June [no year], Ingrid Trobisch Papers.

35. Youngdale, *On My Way Home*, 121–23.

36. Robert, *American Women in Mission*, 416.

37. Youngdale, *On My Way Home*, 129. Although Walter's *J'ai Aimé Une Fille* (1962) was in circulation before Ingrid's *On Our Way Rejoicing* (1964), the latter was the first of the Trobisches' books to be published by a major publishing house.

learned a tremendous amount about writing from working with Ingrid's editor, Edward Sammis. Ingrid's relationship with Sammis and Melvin Arnold at Harper & Row was helpful in getting several of their future books published.

Around the time that Ingrid began working on her book, the Trobisches also began experiencing doubts about their work at Libamba. In 1956, when Walter had agreed to take the position, he and Ingrid had been proud to be part of the institution that would supply "the future teachers, lawyers, doctors and pastors" in Cameroon.[38] They also saw the strategic importance of their post as missionaries at Libamba. They believed that giving the young people of Cameroon a Christian education would influence the future of Cameroon. However, by October of 1961, the Trobisches were more pessimistic, even cynical, about what they were doing at Libamba. They came to believe that the only reason many students were Christian was because the students saw it as the best way of achieving wealth and status. Therefore, missionaries like themselves were essentially "advancing materialism instead of the Gospel."[39]

The gravity of the situation was highlighted for them when Walter preached a number of sermons on the Incarnation, the notion that God "became flesh and dwelt among us."[40] Walter urged the students to let God dwell among them by using African styles of worship in church. Instead of "amens" he received a constant stream of loud clicks, "the sign of uttermost disapproval." When questioning a student about it after the service, the student told him, "If you say, 'Don't imitate us!' that means to us as much as if you would say: 'I do not want you to reach our level of learning and living, but wish rather that you remain uncivilized savages.'"[41] To many of the students at Libamba, Christianity was simply part and parcel of becoming civilized.

As Walter Trobisch continued to interact with students at Libamba and learn more about the Protestant churches in Cameroon, he realized that he was looking for indigenization in the wrong places. African Christians were hesitant to use African music in church, but there was a different kind of indigenization going on, nonetheless. When Trobisch looked at the widespread use of church discipline (excommunication, prohibition from taking communion, fines) in African churches, he saw something peculiar to the African church. Trobisch argued that while paternalistic missionaries were

---

38. W. and I. Trobisch to friends, June 1956, Ingrid Trobisch Papers.
39. W. and I. Trobisch to friends, October 1961, Walter Trobisch Collection, Box 12.
40. John 1:14.
41. W. and I. Trobisch to friends, October 1961, Walter Trobisch Collection, Box 12.

partially to blame for the widespread use of church discipline in Africa, the extensive use of church discipline also developed because it fit well with African conceptions of authority. As Trobisch saw it, the parish priest had replaced the tribal chief. The community gave the priest ultimate authority to dispense judgment and punishment, rather than leaving this to God.

Trobisch's examination of church discipline led him to an important discovery. He found that "95 percent of all punishments meted out by the church are for adultery."[42] Clearly, Christian marriage in Africa was not as it should be. Trobisch realized that missionaries and Africans often had opposing ideas about love and sex. "Whereas for the African love spends itself in sex, for the pietistic missionary sex is often identified with sin."[43] Trobisch knew of no missionary or African pastor who had tried to address this issue. When missionaries and African pastors spoke about sex, it was in order to condemn adultery. He knew of no one in Africa who had tried to articulate a positive view of sex from a Christian perspective.

MARRIAGE COUNSELING AT LIBAMBA

Walter Trobisch's beliefs were reinforced by conversations he had with students. As chaplain, he had been discussing issues of love, sex, and marriage with students since he had arrived at Libamba. While teaching German, preaching in chapel, and supervising meals brought him endless frustration, individual conversations with students brought him great satisfaction. Unlike the students Trobisch had worked with in Europe, his African students were not shy about discussing their personal lives and were receptive to the counsel he offered.

> Never will an African refuse to come if you invite him for a counseling talk. An American or European boy would feel hurt. For an African boy there is nothing humiliating about it. It is natural for him to be counseled. Having grown up in a society which took notice of him only as a member of a collective group, it is an honour for him to be invited personally, to be taken ... as an individual. He will not miss that chance and he will bring two things along which occidental youth normally does not have: time and readiness to listen.[44]

42. Trobisch, "Church Discipline in Africa," 202.

43. Trobisch, "Church Discipline in Africa," 202.

44. W. Trobisch, "Soul Counselling with African Youth," Walter Trobisch Collection, Box 12, Folder 39.

Trobisch had long been passionate about counseling. His first set of lectures for the annual conference of the Sudan Mission back in 1954 had been on soul-counseling. These had been so well received that he had sent out excerpts in the form of letters to his fellow missionaries the following year. But it was not until Libamba that Trobisch really had a chance to put his passion for counseling into practice. And by doing so, he changed the course of his and Ingrid's life.

The more Trobisch met with students, the more he and Ingrid came to believe that "one of their greatest needs today—and perhaps at the same time the greatest contribution the Christian church can make to Africa—is for help in the realm of home and family life."[45] Ingrid had first realized the evangelistic potential of sexual guidance while they were living in Tchol-liré. She and her missionary colleague Helen Johnson had begun to teach the women in the village about the biological processes of conception and childbirth. In Libamba, the students were less interested in childbirth and more interested in questions about dating and spouse-selection.

Students at Libamba, like other young Africans who left home for work or education during the mid-twentieth century, experienced a dizzying sense of alienation from their families and traditional way of life.[46] In most rural African societies, the elders of the community essentially controlled the community's economy. As young people moved to cities for work or education, they found that the modern, free-market economy enabled them to obtain a job without the aid of their family. Traditional African societies were marked by a "corporate existence" in which young people were surrounded by members of their kin group.[47] Young people could count on family members to defend them or bail them out when they got into trouble. Siblings were readily present who could run an errand for them or investigate a potential spouse's family. Living away from home, young people had none of these benefits of corporate life. African theologian John Mbiti argued in 1970 that this separation from corporate life caused young people to "float in life like a cloud."[48]

These young people faced numerous social situations for which they were unprepared. In traditional African cultures, a person would marry the spouse whom the family had carefully selected. Interaction with a potential

---

45. Trobisch, *On Our Way Rejoicing,* 205.

46. "Between 1950 and 1985, the urban population in Africa increased from 20 million to 127 million" (Oheneba-Sakyi and Takyi, "Introduction to the Study of African Families," 15).

47. Mba and Bangha, "Reflections on the Changing Family System in Cameroon," 184–85.

48. Mbiti, *African Religions and Philosophy,* 219.

spouse was strictly monitored by custom and family oversight. But when young people relocated for work or education, these structures fell away. A young man in the city might live next to or attend class with a woman who struck his fancy. He might casually get to know her, invite her over to his place, have sexual relations with her, and decide to marry her, all without his parents' consent. The desire to choose one's own spouse was a result not only of the conditions of urban life but also of a Western education, which emphasized individualism.[49] As increasing numbers of men and women gained access to education and encountered each other in the school environment, it was natural for romantic relationships to develop. The social norms these young people had grown up with in the village did not seem to apply to their new romantic encounters, and parents and elders could offer little by way of advice.

The students at Libamba were hungry for conversations about love, sex, and marriage. They wanted to know why the church forbid premarital sex and why it favored monogamy over polygamy. They wanted to discuss what love was and how it was related to sex. The Trobisches began gathering materials that would help them answer the students' questions. Ingrid later wrote in her autobiography, "Together we would sit by the kerosene lamp of our dining table and discuss for hours how these questions might best be addressed. How could we make abstract concepts real and practical?"[50] A missionary linguist and fellow lecturer at Libamba, William D. Reyburn, also remembered discussing the questions with Walter. "We spent many hours together, particularly in the company of some of his students, talking about and searching the significance of polygamous marriages, brideprice payments, arranged marriages, circumcision, and many other social practices that impinged on his students' lives. We traveled together spending days on the roads, never tiring of the topics of our conversations."[51]

The Trobisches decided to develop a course on marriage to explore Christian and African concepts of love, sex, and marriage. Walter taught the upper-level boys, in groups of "not more than fifteen in number."[52] Ingrid taught the girls. As the students in Walter's marriage class discussed the meaning of the word "love" in African society, Walter discovered that most of his students associated "love" with sexual intercourse, but not with romance or marital intimacy. His students said things like, "By nature one

49. Mba and Bangha, "Reflections on the Changing Family System in Cameroon," 187.
50. Youngdale, *On My Way Home*, 100.
51. Reyburn, "My Pilgrimage in Mission," 118–19.
52. Trobisch, "Leading Problem," 37.

loves all women and women love all men."⁵³ Another student remarked after taking Walter's marriage class, "Until now, I always thought of love as something cruel." In an article, Trobisch elaborated: "What he [the student] meant was, 'Until now I thought that love was identical with sexuality, and sexuality had only an egotistical and utilitarian purpose.'"⁵⁴

Trobisch came to believe "there was a longing among them for something more, something deeper," but that this desire for romantic love and marital intimacy "had to be awakened, nurtured and unfolded."⁵⁵ Moreover, there were several cultural factors that made the cultivation of romantic love difficult in African society. For one thing, young men and women had no place to casually get to know one another prior to marriage. Without the time to develop a mutual respect for each other prior to marriage, it was consequently more difficult to cultivate intimacy within marriage.

Trobisch thought the bride-price system was one of the greatest obstacles to marital intimacy in Africa. Originally the bride-price had constituted a sum of cattle and other goods and services, which the groom gave to the bride's family.⁵⁶ It compensated her family for the children she would bear, cemented the relationship between the two families, and gave "public recognition to the marriage."⁵⁷ The bride-price was a standard, known quantity of goods, which would not typically change from generation to generation. The bride-price was also originally a safeguard against divorce. In the event that a marriage did not work out, the bride's family had to return the cattle and goods to the groom.⁵⁸ Thus the bride's family had a vested interest in helping the young couple to work out their differences and stay married. In the modern economy, however, the bride-price was increasingly a sum of money, rather than goods or cattle. Furthermore, the amount was not regulated. Often, especially for educated women, fathers demanded so much money that a young man was either forced to go into massive debt or simply not marry.⁵⁹ No longer was the bride-price primarily a means of building community and sustaining marriage. Instead, for many families, it had turned into a quick and easy way of becoming wealthy.

53. Trobisch, "Courtship without Dating," 1.
54. Trobisch, "Pre-Marital Relations," 261.
55. Trobisch, "Courtship without Dating," 2.
56. Goody and Tambiah, *Bridewealth and Dowry*, 1.
57. Oheneba-Sakyi and Takyi, "Introduction to the Study of African Families," 10.
58. Mba and Bangha, "Reflections on the Changing Family System in Cameroon," 181.
59. Doherty, *Role of the African Woman*, 29.

J'AI AIMÉ UNE FILLE

After discussing the bride-price with his students and colleagues at Libamba, Walter Trobisch concluded that something needed to be done. "What was needed in Cameroun was to give the word 'love' a new meaning and to do something effective against the abuse of the custom of bride-price."[60] He thought it would be helpful to have something "in writing so we could hand it out to those who came asking for advice."[61] Trobisch knew of no such pamphlet or book, so he began to write one. He had been corresponding about the nature of love, sex, marriage, and the bride-price with a former student. He used this correspondence as a basis for his book. He wrote the book as a series of letters between himself and this former student and called the book *J'ai Aimé Une Fille* (I Loved a Girl), deliberately choosing the word *aimé* because it could be used to mean "love" or "sex."

J'ai Aimé Une Fille opened with a young man named François being fired from his teaching position for having premarital sex. In the story, François writes about the situation to his former chaplain, Walter Trobisch. "Last Friday, I loved a girl—or, as you would put it, I committed adultery—at least that's what the whites call it and the Church, too."[62] François argues that he is blameless since "the girl wasn't married, nor had any bride-price been paid for her." Trobisch disagrees and, over the course of several letters, communicates to François that sex belongs in marriage and marriage should be marked by intimate, generous love. Over the course of their correspondence, François tells Trobisch about another young woman he has met, Cecile. François and Cecile end up developing the type of love Trobisch encourages, and the two begin to make plans to be married. However, their dreams are dashed when Cecile's father demands a bride-price of four hundred dollars. The story ends with a letter from François, bitterly decrying the bride-price system and the fact that Trobisch has led him to a dead end: "Four hundred dollars! For me this is altogether out of the question, an impossible amount. You have made me dream. But reality is cruel and destroys that dream. I've ceased to hope."[63]

Trobisch described his booklet as "a pamphlet against the bride-price and a plea for the beauty of marital love."[64] While he was writing *J'ai Aimé Une Fille*, one of his students was writing a play that also dealt with the

---

60. Trobisch, "Courtship without Dating," 3–4.
61. Trobisch, "Courtship without Dating," 4.
62. Trobisch, *Complete Works of Walter Trobisch*, 31.
63. Trobisch, *Complete Works of Walter Trobisch*, 57.
64. Trobisch, "Courtship without Dating," 4.

bride-price and the desire of young people to marry for love. This student, Guillaume Oyono Mbia, went on to publish his play, *Trois Prétendants . . . Un Mari*. In a speech that constitutes the climax of Mbia's play, the main character expresses her frustration with the bride-price system: "Am I to be sold to the highest bidder? Can I not be consulted about my own wedding?"[65]

Trobisch assigned *J'ai Aimé Une Fille* and *Trois Prétendants* as reading for his marriage class during the 1959–1960 school year.[66] He hoped the texts would get a conversation started about love, sex, and marriage in modern Africa. Trobisch's "plea for the beauty of marital love" made such an impression on one of the students in the class, Pierre Oko Mengue, that Mengue wrote to his brother to ask him to find a spouse for him. Mengue's brother selected a woman by the name of Jacqueline Ernestine Bengue Dimodi, who was a classmate of his at the Adventist college in Nanga Eboko, some two hundred kilometers away from Libamba. Mengue and Dimodi exchanged letters and photographs for two years before finally meeting in person in Yaoundé.

When Mengue began to correspond with Dimodi, he immediately told Trobisch about it. Mengue viewed Trobisch as a spiritual guide. The two had been meeting together since Trobisch first arrived at Libamba in 1957. Mengue had grown up in a Christian household. His father was an evangelist, his mother was a deacon, and his grandmother had been the first Christian in her village. Mengue was thus well prepared for the kinds of conversations Trobisch liked to have with students about faith, family, sexuality, sin, and the like. Mengue and about five other students attached themselves to Trobisch as his "disciples," and Trobisch trained this group of disciples to be "sensitive to the slightest sin."[67] Thus when Mengue told him about his correspondence with Dimodi, Trobisch wanted to ensure that the young man was not about to fall into sin. He asked Mengue to show him all the letters he intended to send to Dimodi. Although this strikes the modern reader as paternalistic and personally invasive, Mengue thought the practice of showing his letters to Trobisch was a good one.[68] He appreciated the interest Trobisch took in his spiritual development, and a few years later he appreciated how Trobisch intervened with his family on his behalf. Mengue and Dimodi were from different tribes. Their families, particularly Mengue's mother and Dimodi's brother, were not in support of an intertribal

---

65. Mbia, *Trois Prétendants*, 17–18.
66. Mengue, email, 8 December 2012.
67. Mengue, email, 8 December 2012.
68. Mengue, email, 16 December 2012.

marriage. Trobisch, however, was strongly in favor of the match and did all he could to convince the families that it was a good match.[69]

During the time that Trobisch was reading all of Mengue's letters he was also continuing to revise his own little booklet *J'ai Aimé Une Fille*. It is probable that he incorporated some of the content of Mengue and Dimodi's letters into his own book. In fact, many years later when Mengue and Dimodi were telling the story of their marriage in Caux, Switzerland, a German couple approached them and asked whether they were the couple that Trobisch had written about in his little book *J'ai Aimé Une Fille*. Although *J'ai Aimé Une Fille* was not a straightforward retelling of their story, Mengue and Dimodi feel that Trobisch drew some of his inspiration for *J'ai Aimé Une Fille* from walking beside them during the first year of their engagement. It is also likely that Trobisch drew inspiration from Mbia's *Trois Prétendants* and from conversations he had with other students at Libamba.

Trobisch finished another draft of *J'ai Aimé Une Fille* in 1961. He sent the manuscript to a friend of his in Germany, who offered to donate the paper if Trobisch would pay for the printing. The friend printed three thousand copies of the booklet.[70] The copies of *J'ai Aimé Une Fille* arrived in Cameroon the summer of 1962. Trobisch was in Tanzania teaching on one of his favorite topics: how to use soul-counseling rather than church discipline to solve marital problems. He had arranged for a friend from the Dutch Bible Society to receive the shipment of booklets. The friend "opened one of the packages because he was curious about what was in it. Then he began to sell *J'ai Aimé Une Fille* along with his Bibles in his tiny store."[71] When Trobisch returned from Tanzania and inquired about the booklet, his friend told him that all the copies had been sold. Moreover, people had already asked if the booklet could be translated.

Walter and Ingrid Trobisch quickly made arrangements for a second printing of *J'ai Aimé Une Fille*. This time, they printed ten thousand copies.[72] They began to work on translating the booklet into English and to correspond with Jim Sutton of the United Society for Christian Literature (USCL) to see whether USCL might publish the booklet for English-speaking Africans. Walter also began to work on a sequel to *J'ai Aimé Une Fille*, which would tell "the girls' side of the story."[73]

---

69. Mengue, email, 8 December 2012.
70. Trobisch, *Complete Works of Walter Trobisch*, 16, 724.
71. Trobisch, *Complete Works of Walter Trobisch*, 725.
72. I. Trobisch to Friends, 1 March 1963, Ingrid Trobisch Papers.
73. Ingrid to Co-Workers, 8 December 1962, Ingrid Trobisch Papers.

FROM LIBAMBA TO MANNHEIM

The unexpected success of *J'ai Aimé Une Fille,* just like Ingrid Trobisch's book contract with Harper & Row, served to facilitate the Trobisches' transition into a new kind of mission work. The Trobisches were scheduled to go on furlough in 1963. Walter asked Dr. Syrdal, the Executive Secretary of the ALC Board of Missions, if his one-year furlough salary could be spread over two years. This would allow him to spend some time studying marriage counseling at the University of Heidelberg. Increasingly, it was becoming clear to Walter that marriage counseling, not teaching German and Bible at Libamba, was his true vocation. This had become evident through the years of teaching his marriage course at Libamba and had been confirmed when he taught on Christian marriage at Makumira Theological Seminary in July of 1962.

In the summer of 1962, Walter's poor health was another sign that the Trobisches' work at Libamba might be coming to an end. Ingrid had long been worried about Walter's ill health at Libamba. In a letter drafted but never sent to the mission board, she described Walter's poor state of health: "More than ever before he's been burning the candle at both ends, in an attempt to keep up with his school obligations as well as all the correspondence and writing tasks awaiting him. . . . I was afraid he couldn't keep it up past Christmas. . . . And then this week it happened. Walter simply said that he could not teach another class at Libamba, and he stayed in bed—and that's where he's been the last four days. . . . All desire and will to continue here has left him."[74] The nature of Walter's work at Libamba and the sheer workload had bothered him since he had started at the school in 1956, but each time he and Ingrid had discussed the matter they had decided to acquiesce to the mission board and stay at Libamba. Even when Walter felt he lacked a personal "call" to the work at hand, he and Ingrid had managed to summon the strength to go on, for the sake of the mission and for their own sake, lest they "jeopardize our mid-term furlough."[75] But between Walter's breakdown in the summer of 1962, his growing desire to explore African marital issues, and the opportunity that had arisen to study at the University of Heidelberg, he and Ingrid no longer felt any resolve to stay at Libamba.

The Libamba School Board agreed to release Walter Trobisch from his teaching contract in January of 1963, and the ALC mission board granted Trobisch a two-year study leave for 1963 and 1964. Trobisch happily devoted himself to writing projects in January of 1963. In February he went

---

74. I. Trobisch to Dr. Syrdal, no date, Ingrid Trobisch Papers.
75. I. Trobisch, Journal, 3 February 1960, Ingrid Trobisch Papers.

to Kitwe, northern Rhodesia (now Zambia) to serve as chaplain and to represent Cameroon at the All-Africa Seminar on the Christian Home and Family Life. Meanwhile, Ingrid flew to Frankfurt, Germany with their three youngest children. One of Walter's former students, Jean Banyolak, went with them and stayed on to study marriage counseling in Germany.[76] Ingrid left four-year-old David with Walter's mother in Mannheim and three-year-old Stephen with another family. Taking two-year-old Ruth with her, she flew to London, where she met with Jim Sutton of the United Society for Christian Literature (USCL) to discuss whether the USCL might publish *J'ai Aimé Une Fille* in English for English-speaking Africans. From there, she went on to New York to discuss her own book with Edward Sammis and Melvin Arnold of Harper & Row. Finally, she flew to Springfield, Missouri, where she hoped to finish her book while staying at her mother's house.

The Trobisches planned to reunite as a family in Germany on May 1. "But then everything went wrong."[77] Little Stephen cried for two weeks straight after Ingrid left. Rosemarie, the mother who was caring for him, broke her arm. Rosemarie's husband wrote to Ingrid to say Rosemarie could no longer take care of Stephen; Ingrid would have to return to retrieve him.[78] But Ingrid had just had an operation and could not travel. Stephen could not go to stay with Walter's mother because she had the flu. So Stephen was taken to a children's home in the Black Forest. As Ingrid dryly remarked in a letter to friends, "What a paradox—Walter lecturing on Christian family life at the All-Africa Conference in Rhodesia and I trying to write a story which would be a testimony of how one family lived out their Christian faith—and our own little family had to pay the price."[79]

Walter Trobisch ended up leaving the All-Africa Conference early. He picked up their two oldest children, Katrine and Daniel, at their school in Garoua-Boulaï, Cameroon. Then he flew to Germany, where he picked up David and Stephen. Then they flew to Springfield, via Chicago.[80] The Trobisches were together as a family in Springfield from April to September of 1963. Energized by the fact that the second edition of *J'ai Aimé Une Fille* was "going just as fast and reaching into all parts of French-speaking West Africa," Walter continued working on the sequel, which he decided to call *I*

---

76. Trobisch and Trobisch, *Adventures of Pumpelhoober*, 44–46.
77. Trobisch and Trobisch, *Adventures of Pumpelhoober*, 47.
78. [no name] to Ingrid, 15 February 1963, Ingrid Trobisch Papers.
79. I. Trobisch to friends, 20 May 1963, Ingrid Trobisch Papers.
80. David Trobisch humorously tells the story of this trip in *The Adventures of Pumpelhoober*.

Love a Young Man.[81] Ingrid tried to write three pages of her book each day, though this was difficult with the five children to care for.[82]

In September of 1963, Walter went to Germany to find an apartment for the family, enroll their oldest son in school, and begin his own studies at the University of Heidelberg.[83] Six months later, in March of 1964, the rest of the family joined Walter and Danny in Germany. It was an exciting time for the Trobisches. Both Ingrid and Walter had a book in print. Their family was together again, settled for the time being in a four room apartment in Mannheim.[84] And demands for the translation rights to *J'ai Aimé Une Fille* continued to pour in.

J'AI AIMÉ UNE FILLE IN SEVENTY LANGUAGES

Between 1962 and 1973, *J'ai Aimé Une Fille* was translated into seventy languages and one million copies of the book were printed.[85] Many of the earliest translations of *J'ai Aimé Une Fille* were into various African languages. In her summary of the translations of *J'ai Aimé Une Fille*, Ingrid Trobisch listed the following African translations, occasionally noting the number of copies that had been printed:

> Swahili (25,000), Luganda (5000), Runyankore (3000), Sessouto (5000), Shona (5000), Zulu (?), Bulu (Cameroun), Bassa (Cameroun), Lingala (Congo), Chinvania (S. Rhodesia). A Burakeye translation has been printed in serial form in Burundi and the same is true of Yoruba where it was printed in the "Yoruba Challenge" in Nigeria.[86]

Walter Trobisch used the missionary infrastructure in Africa to get his book on the shelves of Christian bookstores and into the hands of young readers. For example, when Elsie Suh, an 18-year-old in English-speaking West Cameroon, wrote Trobisch requesting a copy of *J'ai Aimé Une Fille* in English, he took the opportunity to ask whether she would help him make the book more readily available in West Cameroon. Suh had presumably

---

81. I. Trobisch to Friends, 1 March 1963, Ingrid Trobisch Papers.
82. Youngdale, *On My Way Home*, 126.
83. I. Trobisch to Messengers, 12 February 1964, Ingrid Trobisch Papers.
84. W. and I. Trobisch to friends, July 1966, Missionary Personnel Files.
85. For a fuller description of the translation history, see Stasson, "Love, Sex, and Marriage," 116–30.
86. A list of all the editions of *J'ai Aimé Une Fille* either published or in progress, Walter Trobisch Collection, Box 12, "Heidelberg" folder.

read a copy of the book owned either by a friend or by her school, Saker Baptist College in Victoria. Trobisch asked her to

> go to a Christian bookstore in Victoria or talk to your missionaries and those especially who are in charge of literature, and urge them to order that booklet in great quantities. They can get quite a reduction and then make even some profit on it. I sold already close to 30,000 booklets over there in French Cameroun, and I am very surprised that so far nobody actually has reacted in the English speaking side of Cameroun. Please, show your missionaries this letter, your literature secretaries may be African or European. See whether you find a Christian bookstore in Victoria, and tell them what this booklet meant to you, and urge them to make a bulk order.[87]

Suh presumably complied with Trobisch's request because a subsequent letter told him, "The book is now available in the Basel Mission Bookshop Victoria."[88]

What is most interesting about *J'ai Aimé Une Fille* is that it found a readership far beyond Africa. According to Ingrid Trobisch, six publishing houses requested rights to publish *J'ai Aimé Une Fille* in German. The Trobisches finally chose the press "who fought the hardest for it and whom we felt understood its inner message."[89] By 1966, the Trobisches could proudly write in their newsletter, "160,000 have been printed to date in Germany, putting it at the head of the list as far as religious paper-backs are concerned."[90]

German author Ruth Heil read the book when she was a teenager in the 1960s. "It was the first book in all the Christian bookstores around, which talked very clearly in a wonderful way about the thinking of man and woman," she remembers.[91] Heil and other young people like her found the book immanently helpful as they contemplated their sexual feelings and choices.

During the 1960s and 1970s, *J'ai Aimé Une Fille* appeared in every major European language. It was also translated into Nabak (a language of

---

87. Elsie Suh to W. Trobisch, 25 June 1964, Walter Trobisch Collection, Box 15, Folder S.

88. This message is scribbled at the bottom of a letter from Dot Dolly Kofo Anjolin to W. Trobisch, no date, filed with Elsie Suh, Walter Trobisch Collection, Box 15, Folder S. The message is signed by Alice Suh, another student at Saker Baptist College and presumably a relative of Elsie Suh.

89. I. Trobisch to Edward Sammis, 23 November 1964, Ingrid Trobisch Papers.

90. W. and I. Trobisch to dear ones, 10 May 1966, Ingrid Trobisch Papers.

91. R. Heil, email, 22 March 2010.

Papua New Guinea), Korean, Chinese, Japanese, Indonesian, Thai, Tagalog, Hindi, Telagu, Oriya (another Indian language), and several Semitic languages, including Amharic, Hebrew, and Tigrinya. Most editions of *J'ai Aimé Une Fille* were published by religious presses. With sexual norms being in such a state of flux and the church scrambling to make its stance on premarital chastity clear and convincing, religious presses jumped at the chance to publish a book that advocated a distinctly Christian view of love, sex, and marriage and that had already proven popular among young people in other countries.

In the United States *J'ai Aimé Une Fille* was first published in serial form in *HIS* magazine (circulation 20,000), a publication of the campus ministry InterVarsity Christian Fellowship. According to *HIS* editor Paul Fromer, the magazine "received more reader response from this series than from any material published in that year in *HIS*."[92] Owing to this positive response, Harper & Row published the first combined edition of *I Loved a Girl* and its sequel *I Loved a Young Man* in 1965.

---

92. List of all the editions of *J'ai Aimé Une Fille* either published or in progress, Walter Trobisch Collection, Box 12, "Heidelberg" folder.

3

Marriage Counseling by Mail from the Austrian Alps

In 1962, when Walter Trobisch first wrote *J'ai Aimé Une Fille,* he had no idea that it would reach young people all across Africa, not to mention Europe, Asia, North America, and South America. In 1964, when the Trobisches relocated to Mannheim, Germany, they were beginning to get a sense of a wider interest in the book, but their primary focus remained on Africa. They had come to Mannheim so Walter could dedicate his time to analyzing marital practices in Africa. As he did so, a constant stream of letters from Africans who had seen his address on the back of *J'ai Aimé Une Fille* arrived. The Trobisches enlisted the help of several other people, obtained funding, and established Marriage Guidance Service for Africa, a ministry that enabled them to answer all the letters. The Africans who wrote to Walter Trobisch found in him a welcome confidant and guide. These young people were already committed to modern marital practices like spouse self-selection and marrying for love but had particular questions related to their own unique situations. Some were also looking for ways to bring their Christian faith into conversation with modern forms of sexuality and marriage.

MARRIAGE GUIDANCE SERVICE FOR AFRICA

In April of 1964, Walter Trobisch told a friend that he was receiving letters "from over 20 different countries."[1] He would later reflect that because the

---

1. W. Trobisch to John Beunde, 14 April 1964, Walter Trobisch Collection, Box 14.

book was written as a series of letters, "Africans drew three conclusions from the book: (1) Walter Trobisch must be a man who reads letters; (2) he takes them seriously; (3) why couldn't he answer me too?"[2] By 1965, Trobisch had received "more than one thousand letters."[3] He and a team of "four part-time secretaries" answered the letters.[4] One of these secretaries, Hans-Joachim Heil, played a particularly important role in the work. As a theology student, proficient in Hebrew, Aramaic, and Greek, he functioned as a kind of "Melanchthon for Martin Luther," helping Trobisch think through some of the theological questions he encountered in his work.[5] Trobisch also trained Heil to answer the letters, eventually trusting Heil to write the letters and sign them with Trobisch's name. While Heil answered the letters from Africa, Trobisch answered the letters that came from Europe and America. Handing over the Africa correspondence also enabled Trobisch to work on further books for the African context, travel to speaking engagements, and work on his degree at Heidelberg. Heil remembers feeling strange the first time he signed a letter in Trobisch's name, but he ultimately believed that "since Walter had trained me and since he read and approved the copies I sent him, these were indeed 'his' letters."[6]

The Trobisches, Jean Banyolak (Walter's former student who had come to Europe to study), and the various part-time secretaries who helped with the work named their venture Marriage Guidance Service for Africa (MGSA) and obtained grants from several organizations to support the work.[7] In the spring of 1965, the Trobisches moved from Mannheim to the Lichtenberg, "a mountain firmly bedded in the Upper Austrian foothills of the Alps."[8] The father of a friend of Walter's had promised to give Walter land someday.[9] Walter had contacted the friend's father when he first returned to Germany. The man gave the Trobisches a beautiful plot of land with a breathtaking view of the Alps. The Trobisches erected a simple, prefabricated home there among the homes of four farmers.[10] This became the headquarters of MGSA, and the one salaried secretary for MGSA, Ruth

2. Trobisch, *Complete Works of Walter Trobisch*, 725.
3. Banyolak, "Africa Needs Marriage Counsellors," 67.
4. W. Trobisch to John Beunde, 14 April 1964, Walter Trobisch Collection, Box 14.
5. R. Heil, email, 21 March 2010.
6. H. Heil, email, 22 November 2011.
7. Banyolak, "Africa Needs Marriage Counsellors," 69.
8. Youngdale, *On My Way Home*, 69.
9. Danzer, interview, 18 August 2012.
10. W. Trobisch to John Beunde, 7 June 1966, Walter Trobisch Collection, Box 14.

Kamerzell, lived with them in their home.[11] During the school year, the younger children walked to the village school four miles away. The older children attended a boarding school in Salzburg, coming home a couple weekends a month.

From the founding of MGSA in 1965 until Walter's sudden death in 1979, the Trobisches and the various others who were involved in MGSA and its successor, Family Life Mission, carried on a marriage counseling correspondence ministry with Africans. By 1973, they had received 9,000 letters, and in 1974, the Trobisches told a Minneapolis newspaper that they had received 10,000 letters.[12] While some of these letters came from people who had met Walter Trobisch in person, most of them came from people who had read *J'ai Aimé Une Fille* and had decided to write to him about personal problems of their own.

AN OFFER OF GUIDANCE AND VALIDATION OF COMPLEXITY

Urbanization and the consequent alienation of young people from traditional sources of authority formed the context for the enthusiastic response of young people to *J'ai Aimé Une Fille*. When they read the text, they felt understood. Twenty-one-year-old C. Tanmi of Cameroon told Walter Trobisch, "The whole book seems to be dealing with my personal difficulties."[13] A. Mitchell from Liberia wrote to Trobisch after reading *J'ai Aimé Une Fille*, "Please have this in mind dear Pastor, don't think that the advice you and your wife give to François and Cecile were just for the both of them. I can say this I was really in need of those advices."[14] These young people also felt that Trobisch would somehow be able to help them sort out the relational issues in their lives. "I've been long burning with problems, not knowing to whom will I find advice. But God has heard my call and has brought you to my rescue," wrote

---

11. Walter's mother, Mutti, also lived with them until her death in 1967 ("The Lichtenberg-Ten" to "Dear Ones," 10 May 1966, Ingrid Trobisch Papers). The Trobisches also usually had someone living with them as "Haustochter and Kinderschwester" (house daughter and nanny).

12. Walter Trobisch Collection, Box 20; Trobisch, *Complete Works of Walter Trobisch*, 725.

13. C. Tanmi to W. Trobisch, June 1965, Walter Trobisch Collection, Box 15, Folder T.

14. A. Mitchell to W. Trobisch, 15 August 1966, Walter Trobisch Collection, Box 15, Folder M.

G. Mashaba of South Africa.[15] "I am perplexed and don't know what to do. I need your help," wrote a Ghanaian woman.[16]

Seeking advice about sex and marriage was an entrenched part of African culture, most often handled during the traditional coming-of-age rituals, but neither those rituals nor a modern education prepared African young people for the sexual and marital issues they faced in the modern world. Reading *J'ai Aimé Une Fille* and corresponding with Trobisch helped young people sort through both their cultural heritage and the colonial heritage. In their letters, they worked out what to keep and what to jettison as they made their way in modern, independent Africa.

Some readers of *J'ai Aimé Une Fille* wrote to Trobisch to confess sin and obtain forgiveness. "I am convinced that you are the person whom I so long longed to confess to," wrote E. Prince.[17] "I am writing to you with a heavy and anguished heart. I am writing to you because I hope you would understand, because I cannot keep it to myself any longer and I cannot trust anybody with it; because it is too shameful," wrote R. Lomotey of Ghana.[18]

Trobisch did not belittle his counselees by suggesting that there were easy answers to their problems. On the contrary, *J'ai Aimé Une Fille* ended with François's despairing words, "I do not expect an answer, for there is none." Even when Trobisch wrote the sequel to *J'ai Aimé Une Fille*, the book ended in tragedy. In the story, Cecile's father accepts the bride-price from another suitor.[19] Since François and Cecile have not yet accumulated the money for the bride-price, they choose to elope so that Cecile will not be forced to marry the other suitor. The story ends with Cecile being sick in bed, having "caught a bad cold the night we ran away."[20] François and Cecile cannot find a way to balance their desire to marry for love and their desire to honor kin. They have to choose one ideal over the other. This kind of bittersweet ending validated the emotions many young people felt about the relational problems in their own lives.

J'ai Aimé Une Fille did not simplify the problems of modern Africa because Walter Trobisch knew the problems could not be simplified. An African bishop of the Lutheran Church in Liberia would later write of Trobisch,

15. G. Mashaba to I. Trobisch, 17 October 1966, Walter Trobisch Collection, Box 15, Folder M.

16. A. Frimpona to W. Trobisch, 29 October 1968, Walter Trobisch Collection, Box 14, Folder F.

17. E. Prince to W. Trobisch, 4 July 1966, Walter Trobisch Collection, Box 15, Folder P.

18. R. Lomotey to W. Trobisch, 6 December 1965, Walter Trobisch Collection, Box 14, Folder L.

19. Trobisch, *Complete Works of Walter Trobisch*, 110.

20. Trobisch, *Complete Works of Walter Trobisch*, 111.

"He is one of the few non-Africans who can communicate and have a dialog with the African."[21] Trobisch's children would later point out that many who read his book simply assumed he was African.[22]

ENDORSEMENT OF PREMARITAL CHASTITY

One of the issues that arose frequently in the letters Trobisch received was the question of how to express sexual feelings prior to marriage. The process of urbanization and the separation of young people from the ethical norms that governed rural life led to an increase in premarital sex.[23] The letters Trobisch received testified that some young people were disillusioned with premarital sexual relations in modern Africa and were interested in pursuing a stricter ethical code.

E. Suh, an eighteen-year-old from Cameroon, wrote to Trobisch about her strong sexual temptations. She then thanked him for the advice he offered in *J'ai Aimé Une Fille* on how to stay chaste.[24] A. Mitchell thanked Trobisch for coming down hard on the African idea that young men should prove their sexual virility before marriage, lest they be considered a "dishcloth." She wrote, "What happened to François is the same things that go around here but instead of calling the boy a dishcloth they call him a boyscout."[25]

In Trobisch's eyes, the Christian ethic of premarital chastity was primarily about helping people maintain their sense of dignity and self-respect.[26] This message particularly struck H. S. Muhemebet of Ethiopia. Prior to reading *J'ai Aimé Une Fille* Muhemebet had been infatuated with one of her classmates, despite the fact that when the two of them were "alone he tries to induce me to have sexual relations with him."[27] Reading *J'ai Aimé Une Fille* made Muhemebet reconsider her affection for the young man. In her letter, she asked Trobisch, "Do you think that this boy wanted my

---

21. Payne, "Reactions and Echoes to Family Life Seminars."
22. S. Trobisch, interview, 5 September 2010.
23. Pauw, *Second Generation*, 137.
24. E. Suh to W. Trobisch, 28 May 1964, Walter Trobisch Collection, Box 15, Folder S.
25. A. Mitchell to W. Trobisch, 15 August 1966, Walter Trobisch Collection, Box 15, Folder M. François had said he had to prove his sexual virility so that his friends would not make fun of him or call him a "dishrag," which he said was a word "we use in our tribal language to describe a man who is both cowardly and impotent" (Trobisch, *Complete Works of Walter Trobisch*, 41).
26. W. Trobisch to R. Lomotey, 12 February 1966, Walter Trobisch Collection, Box 14, Folder L.
27. H. S. Muhemebet to W. Trobisch, no date, Walter Trobisch Collection, Box 15, Folder M.

company in order to satisfy his need whenever it is convenient for him?" At the close of the letter she wrote, "After I read your book I decided not to keep company of any men who want to have a sexual relation with me." Reading the letter, it seems that Trobisch's endorsement of premarital chastity in *J'ai Aimé Une Fille* caused Muhemebet to gain a new sense of her own self-worth and to change her mind regarding the classmate.

ENDORSEMENT OF SPOUSE SELF-SELECTION, MARRYING FOR LOVE, AND COMPANIONATE MARRIAGE

Another message of *J'ai Aimé Une Fille* that struck a chord with those who read it was its advocacy of spouse self-selection. Increasingly, young people of the period were embarking on their own quest to find a spouse, just as Trobisch's student Pierre Oko Mengue had done. Numerous studies from the mid-twentieth century noted the increasing numbers of young people arranging their own marriages and marrying for love.[28] A study conducted in Cameroon in the early 1970s found that one-third of women under the age of thirty and almost one-third of men under the age of thirty spoke about the importance of love in male-female relationships. This was significant, considering the fact that only one-tenth of the women over the age of thirty spoke about the importance of love.[29] In traditional African societies, emotional intimacy was not the primary purpose of marriage. Rather, "the greatest stress was laid upon the group significance and procreative purpose of marriage."[30] By the 1960s, young couples in Africa were increasingly interested in a marriage with more emotional intimacy, as well as a sense of equality.[31]

Trobisch went as far as to argue that an equal relationship between men and women in marriage would help the political independence movement. "Man cannot be free as long as there is no free woman at his side. Political independence is not possible without independent and responsible couples. But there will be no independent couples as long as love is not the supporting foundation of marriage."[32] Trobisch's argument seems rhetorical more

---

28. Lawrence, *Iteso*, 94; Banton, *West African City*, 208; Mbiti, *Love and Marriage in Africa*, 225–26.

29. Weekes-Vagliani, *Family Life and Structure in Southern Cameroon*, 39–43.

30. Hastings, *Christian Marriage in Africa*, 30.

31. Lloyd, *Africa in Social Change*, 30; Little, "Attitudes Towards Marriage and the Family," 149.

32. Trobisch, *Complete Works of Walter Trobisch*, 61.

than anything. And it is unlikely that Africans adopted a Western model of courtship and marriage so as to facilitate their independence movement. However, the fact that independence was underway and that young, urban Africans were poised to become the future leaders of their countries does have something to say about why these same individuals began marrying for love and treating their spouse as an equal. Educated, urban society was infused with the longing for and the language of political and economic freedom. It was natural for this longing to infiltrate the arena of personal relationships. And it was natural for young men and women to begin to use the language of rights to describe their personal relationships. For example, when several African women attended an international congress of Catholic women in October of 1957, "They insisted upon recognition of their equality with men as human persons, their equal dignity and their equal fundamental human rights . . . before, during, and after marriage."[33]

The growing interest in love as a basis for marriage was something that Trobisch had noticed while teaching at Libamba. His description of love in *J'ai Aimé Une Fille* had appealed to his students, and it continued to appeal to those who later read the book. Trobisch stressed the difference between love and sex and highlighted the way in which intimacy and personal sacrifice were integral to love. Trobisch's description of love resonated strongly with those who read his book. It inspired readers to keep pursuing love as a basis for marriage. F. Tekele from Ethiopia told Trobisch that she had faced the same situation as the characters in *J'ai Aimé Une Fille*. "When I reached the age of nineteen I met my first love (my husband) we use to love and understand each other very deeply, we were very very much in love that we thought we couldn't be apart from each other."[34] Because her parents did not approve of the marriage, the two eloped. "My parents didn't know about it, all the world was against us, but we were still happy and faithful to each other, because there was love between us, so every thing was bearable."

Trobisch believed that marriages based on love were essential for full human flourishing. Most of the young Africans who wrote to him wholeheartedly agreed.[35] A. Suh of Cameroon told Trobisch that while her peers wanted "to marry either a rich man or a well educated man," she wanted to marry George simply because she loved him and believed he was "the one God has chosen for me."[36] T. Bogale of Ethiopia told Trobisch that

33. Marie André du Sacré Cœur, *House Stands Firm*, 228.

34. F. Tekele to W. Trobisch, 17 November 1966, Walter Trobisch Collection, Box 15, Folder T.

35. N. Tangwan to I. Trobisch, 23 February 1966, Walter Trobisch Collection, Box 15, Folder T.

36. A. Suh to W. Trobisch, 17 April 1968, Walter Trobisch Collection, Box 15,

he loved a girl "more than any body on the earth. I will never marry another girl if I cannot marry her."[37] The problem for Bogale was that he did not trust the woman he loved. He felt she had betrayed him by dating other men and lying to him about it. "I love her truly and my love to her is not a hidden treasure—I usually reveal it to her and to others as well; but I feel that I am not equally loved," he wrote. J. Ngbede Elijah of Nigeria had a similar problem. The woman he loved and expected to marry had left him. He wrote to Trobisch, "How I wish I forget her, but it seems that when she left that day along with her she took my heart, if so how can I love another when my heart is somewhere far away? She taught me to love her and now she has gone."[38]

N. Tangwan of Cameroon told Trobisch that she loved two boys, both of whom were interested in marrying her. "The first one who hunted for me has been four years doing medicine in America," she told Trobisch.[39] "There had been a climax of sentiments in our correspondence. Now the writing is just normal but we hope to marry when he comes in June, 1966." The other boy was in Cameroon. Tangwan's father preferred the boy in America, and so did she. The problem was that "the boy in America says he cannot show himself so much [cannot be as expressive in his affection], because he feels that if there is not much sentiment now, there will be no great effect to both of our feelings in case of disappointments." This worried Tangwan. "I am afraid he might leave me when he comes back, but I love him with passion tenderer than the boy here. Which of them do you think will be my husband?" Clearly, Tangwan hoped to marry the boy in America, for whom she felt such tender passion. Knowing Trobisch's endorsement of marrying for love, she wrote for affirmation that following one's heart was the right thing to do, despite the risks involved.

The story of W. Kyereh, a young Ghanaian who wrote to Trobisch, illustrates the way in which membership in the Christian community often provided a context for young people to find a spouse and fall in love. Kyereh met a young woman at church. He told Trobisch that he and the young woman "have been working together for the cause of the Gospel: attending choir practice, service, prayer meetings etc."[40] The two initially became

---

Folder S.

37. T. Bogale to W. Trobisch, 1 April 1967, Walter Trobisch Collection, Box 14, Folder B.

38. J. Ngbede Elijah to W. Trobisch, 12 August 1975, Walter Trobisch Collection, Box 14, Folder E.

39. N. Tangwan to I. Trobisch, 23 February 1966, Walter Trobisch Collection, Box 15, Folder T.

40. W. Kyereh to W. Trobisch, 5 February 1974, Walter Trobisch Collection, Box

interested in each other "as we discussed our problems and shared our joys together." Their friendship progressed, such that Kyereh felt he was able to discuss things "which I cannot otherwise discuss with anybody." He told Trobisch that he had "really fallen in love [with the girl] . . . To confess, she is the girl I really want to be my better half. I can't just imagine what my life will be without her."

Not all of the young people who wrote to Trobisch were like Kyereh, gushing about their romantic relationships. However, even if they had not experienced romantic love themselves, many who wrote to Trobisch desired to do so and refused to acquiesce to marital arrangements that did not originate with romantic love. The experience of M. Bekele from Ethiopia, who carried on a lengthy correspondence with Trobisch in the 1960s, is illustrative of the widespread desire for freedom of choice in marriage. Seventeen-year-old Bekele met a thirty-five-year old man while she was visiting a relative. Her relative simply introduced her to the man, "nothing more." However, "the next day he sent me a letter saying that he wanted to marry me." Bekele said "no," but when the man sent elders to ask her father for her hand in marriage, her father agreed. Bekele telegrammed her brother, who "begged my mother and father to promise not to force me to be engaged."[41] Bekele's letter shows how strongly young people of her generation and education opposed the traditional practice of arranged marriage and desired to be in control of their own decisions. Bekele was not about to allow her parents to marry her off to a man twice her age. She wanted God, not her parents, to help her find a spouse.

DATING ADVICE AND PRAYING FOR A MATE

The young people who wrote to Trobisch wanted to choose their own spouse and marry for love, but many were unsure exactly how to go about meeting a potential spouse. Twenty-year-old L. H. Chikoya of Malawi wrote to Trobisch after his girlfriend of two years broke up with him. He told Trobisch, "I want to start looking for a Life-partner. So I want you to help me."[42] W. Banutalira of Zambia also wrote to ask for help finding a girlfriend. He told Trobisch he was "too shy" and was unable to "express my self to a girl

---

14, Folder K.

41. M. Bekele to W. Trobisch, 26 October 1967, Walter Trobisch Collection, Box 14, Folder B.

42. L. H. Chikoya to W. Trobisch, 15 October 1973, Walter Trobisch Collection, Box 14, Folder C.

because I don't know what I can tell her first and last."[43] Trobisch advised Banutalira to hang out in "a group of girls and boys" or to get himself invited to the home of "a friend who has sisters."[44] In either case, Trobisch said, Banutalira would get himself accustomed to hanging out with girls. Banutalira wrote back a couple years later to thank Trobisch for his advice and to say that it had worked: "I can now tell you that, I meet girls without any difficulty due to your two possibilities."[45]

For other young people, meeting someone to date was not so much the problem as knowing which people were acceptable to date and which were not. In *J'ai Aimé Une Fille,* Trobisch gave advice for how to choose a spouse, but many people still wrote to him for advice pertaining to their particular situation.[46] S. Iyoku, a twenty-five-year-old Bible translator in Nigeria, wrote to Trobisch about his inability to find an appropriate woman to date and marry. "Looking around I can only see children of ten and twelves. Hardly any 15yr old girl has not been married. Also you can not see an educated girl. Every girl is married before she starts schooling."[47] Iyoku wanted to know whether he should simply propose to a child and wait until she came of age or whether he should perhaps marry a widow. He said he did have one friend who was a widow, but he doubted that she was a suitable choice because she was a Roman Catholic. Iyoku was also worried about marrying the widow because she was "bigger than I am and if I marry her, I will be like a house boy to her." Trobisch favored marrying the Roman Catholic widow and tried to assure Iyoku, "You will not be her boy but you will be an equal partner with her. . . . Marrying such a woman would show that it is not the height of the body which counts but the union of the heart."[48]

T. Fosu, a twenty-eight-year-old man from Ghana, also wrote to Trobisch with a question about choosing a spouse. "The problem I am facing to-day is how to choose a wife since I want to marry. I wouldn't like to marry and divorce the wife since it is against Christianity. How can I

---

43. W. Banutalira to W. Trobisch, no date, Walter Trobisch Collection, Box 14, Folder B.

44. W. Trobisch to W. Banutalira, 4 April 1968, Walter Trobisch Collection, Box 14, Folder B.

45. W. Banutalira to W. Trobisch, 8 June 1970, Walter Trobisch Collection, Box 14, Folder B.

46. Trobisch, *Complete Works of Walter Trobisch,* 50–52.

47. S. Iyoku to W. Trobisch, 8 November 1973, Walter Trobisch Collection, Box 14, Folder I.

48. W. Trobisch to S. Iyoku, 13 December 1973, Walter Trobisch Collection, Box 14, Folder I.

know that the girl I intend to marry loves me, obedient and there will be no separation in the years to come?"[49] M. Chulu, a woman from Zambia, was also concerned about choosing the right person to date and marry. "How can I find a proper man to marry in future. I don't mean to go looking for them but when they come to me in which way would I recognize a suitable boy for me? . . . There are many boys who are proposing me at this time, but I am refusing to accept because I don't want any troubles and I don't know how I can accept a right man for me."[50]

Chulu's question was echoed by Bekele, the woman whose brother helped her get out of the engagement to the thirty-five-year old man. Bekele told Trobisch that her "real problem is how to choose the right man."[51] After exchanging several letters with Trobisch, Bekele did start dating someone. She eagerly wrote to Trobisch, "I have met someone whom I think is worth meeting. The first time I met him, writing to you came to mind and I took this opportunity to do so. Two months have elapsed since I met him and we are seeing each other now and then. In other words, I meet him at the University when I go to attend my night classes and he teaches there part time. . . . Remembering your advice, I always pray and ask God to help me work out things in cases like this."[52] Trobisch told Bekele he was "very glad" about her new acquaintance at the university and urged her to continue to rely on God for guidance. "He will surely hear you. For in Psalm 32:8 he has promised: I will instruct you and teach you the way you should go; I will counsel you with my eye upon you."[53]

Trobisch often recommended that counselees pray to God to guide them through the dating process. Prayer was the advice Trobisch gave to J. Kizza, a twenty-one-year-old man from Uganda. Kizza loved a woman who did not seem to return his love.[54] Trobisch told Kizza the signs seemed to suggest that the woman was not the right one for him. Rather, he should "ask God for guidance to show you the right girl who could become your life partner."[55] Kizza appreciated the advice and put it into practice, writing in his

---

49. T. Fosu to W. Trobisch, 6 June 1974, Walter Trobisch Collection, Box 14, Folder F.

50. M. Chulu to W. Trobisch, 17 April 1969, Walter Trobisch Collection, Box 14, Folder C.

51. M. Bekele to W. Trobisch, 26 October 1967, Walter Trobisch Collection, Box 14, Folder B.

52. M. Bekele to W. Trobisch, 29 March 1968, Walter Trobisch Collection, Box 14, Folder B.

53. W. Trobisch to M. Bekele, 21 April 1968, Walter Trobisch Collection, Box 14, Folder B.

54. J. Kizza to W. Trobisch, no date, Walter Trobisch Collection, Box 14, Folder K.

55. W. Trobisch to J. Kizza, 15 December 1969, Walter Trobisch Collection, Box 14,

next letter, "Now I will pray God for his help . . . I feel thanks to God because he has passed in you to help me. Now my heart has settled down well."[56]

J. Kinyanjui, a twenty-one-year-old Kenyan man, also wrote to Trobisch with questions about the dating process. Kinyanjui told Trobisch that he knew many Christian women, but he did not know how to go about dating one of them. "Among the group that I am in there are very many sisters but I don't know how it will work. Will the Lord tell me that it is that one . . . so take her."[57] Trobisch told him to pray about it: "It is never too early to pray for your future wife. Did you already start to do it regularly? Even if you do not yet know her, you can pray that the Lord leads you and her the right way, and that at the right time you will find and know each other."[58] In his next letter, Kinyanjui seemed even more worked up about the difficulties of dating: "One problem here in Africa is that you can't have this thing the whites call dating. . . . Another problem is that . . . there are so many of sisters and you can't know whom is whom for they all seem to have the same actions and attitude towards me."[59] Trobisch again urged Kinyanjui to turn to God:

> I know how difficult it is to find the right partner. That's why I want to turn your eyes to the one who is far more concerned about your choice and happiness than you can be: Jesus. I want you to live in a total inner relaxation knowing that God cares for you . . . It's not primarily your burden to choose or to find the right girl,—it's God's concern to guide you there. So please be confident and quiet and relaxed in your heart. I don't know which way you will find her but the Lord knows![60]

Just as he urged Kinyanjui to pray about his situation, prayer was also the advice Trobisch gave to G. Mashaba of Pretoria when she wrote to him with the following situation: "Please help a little girl of my age. I am 20 years of age, and I am a Christian. I am in love with a certain fellow who is a teacher. I love the fellow, his name is Isaac. He also love me. . . . The only

---

Folder K.

56. J. Kizza to W. Trobisch, 19 January 1970, Walter Trobisch Collection, Box 14, Folder K.

57. J. Kinyanjui to W. Trobisch, 18 January 1978, Walter Trobisch Collection, Box 14, Folder K.

58. W. Trobisch to J. Kinyanjui, 3 March 1978, Walter Trobisch Collection, Box 14, Folder K.

59. J. Kinyanjui to W. Trobisch, 30 January 1979, Walter Trobisch Collection, Box 14, Folder K.

60. W. Trobisch to J. Kinyanjui, 4 May 1979, Walter Trobisch Collection, Box 14, Folder K.

thing that I had realized with Isaac is that he is not a Christian."[61] Mashaba wanted to know whether Trobisch recommended that she break off her relationship with Isaac, since he was not a Christian. Trobisch's response was measured. On one hand, he urged her, "You must continue to pray for Isaac that he will become a Christian. . . . Perhaps God will use your testimony to lead Isaac to Christ."[62] On the other hand, Trobisch warned Mashaba that she "must be ready to sacrifice him—just as Abraham did—if it becomes clear to you that God does not like your being together."

Trobisch made the same point about sacrifice when twenty-five-year-old Y. Beiene of Eritrea wrote to him about his seventeen-year-old fiancé. The two had been secretly engaged for three years. Because the woman had an unmarried elder sister and custom required the elder to marry before the younger, Beiene felt that all he could do was continue to pray for his fiancé and for the increase of their love.[63] He asked if Trobisch would "pray for 'our love' in the name of Heaven." In his response, Trobisch commended Beiene for his prayers: "This really is the best thing you can do and must absolutely have the first place."[64] He assured Beiene "that this girl will be yours in spite of all difficulties if she is the one God has chosen for you." However, Trobisch also challenged Beiene, "Are you willing to give this girl up if this is God's will?" Trobisch told Beiene that if he continued to pray daily, "God will answer your prayers by either strengthening your and her love, or by bringing about . . . a clean break." He told Beiene to be content with whatever path God chose for him, and Beiene seemed to accept this advice, writing in his next letter, "I am very much pleased to get such nice advice which gives mental rest and God's belief. I read your letter several times and . . . I found it to be like some drops of water in a desert which quenches thirst!"[65]

A. Wibaba of Ethiopia also wrote to Trobisch about praying while dating. She told Trobisch that the man she loved had no idea that she loved him. She wondered whether it was "right for me to pray to get him."[66] Trobisch replied,

---

61. G. Mashaba to I. Trobisch, 17 October 1966, Walter Trobisch Collection, Box 15, Folder M.

62. W. Trobisch to G. Mashaba, 6 July 1967, Walter Trobisch Collection, Box 15, Folder M.

63. Y. Beiene to W. Trobisch, 30 September 1971, Walter Trobisch Collection, Box 14, Folder B.

64. W. Trobisch to Y. Beiene, 24 November 1971, Walter Trobisch Collection, Box 14, Folder B.

65. Y. Beiene to W. Trobisch, 1 December 1971, Walter Trobisch Collection, Box 14, Folder B.

66. A. Wibaba to I. Trobisch, no date, Walter Trobisch Collection, Box 15, Folder W.

Concerning the pastor you love . . . He probably has no idea whatsoever about your interest in him. The first thing you should do is to find out through some friends whether he has someone else he loves. If he does not you must try to get somehow to get in contact with him. Maybe you can arrange to be invited to a party or to a home where he is also invited. In that way you would have to try to get acquainted with him and to call your attention to him. This is not at all a sin for a girl to do that.[67]

Being encouraged to take such an active role in pursuing a man must have meshed well with Wibaba's conception of herself. Her letter reveals that she already had a fairly independent conception of herself, despite the fact that she had so far lacked the confidence to initiate a relationship with the pastor.[68]

Just as he had told Wibaba to be more assertive, so Trobisch told P. Kagotho, a twenty-seven-year-old Kenyan man, to be more assertive. Kagotho told Trobisch that he had been praying for a spouse "for about 10 years." He went on, "Even when I was a young kid of about 15 years I was praying God about the same issue. Up to now I have not found God's answer to my prayer. . . . Now I really want a wife not a girlfriend."[69] In his response, Trobisch told Kagotho that rather than simply waiting for God to present him with a wife, he should "look around in [his] church, or among the relatives of [his] friends. . . . Sometimes we expect God to do great miracles, but indeed we simply have to do a very small step in faith. It's not always God who has to act, but sometimes we have to act."[70] A year later Kagotho wrote again to tell Trobisch that he had finally found a girlfriend: "I have really prayed God to help me. . . . I have followed your advice just as you told me and at last I am successful."[71]

R. Klu, a twenty-two-year-old man from Ghana, also wrote to Trobisch about prayer in the context of dating. Klu's correspondence demonstrates the role of prayer not only in finding and choosing a spouse but also

---

67. W. Trobisch to A. Wibaba, 14 November 1968, Walter Trobisch Collection, Box 15, Folder W.

68. She wrote, "If ever God wants me to marry I would like a man who will be interested to work with me in my church because my church counts a lot on me" (A. Wibaba to W. Trobisch, no date, Walter Trobisch Collection, Box 15, Folder W).

69. P. Kagotho to W. Trobisch, 12 May 1973 and 5 January 1974, Walter Trobisch Collection, Box 14, Folder K.

70. W. Trobisch to P. Kagotho, 28 January 1974, Walter Trobisch Collection, Box 14, Folder K.

71. P. Kagotho to W. Trobisch, 18 April 1975, Walter Trobisch Collection, Box 14, Folder K.

in dealing with disappointment during the dating process. When Klu first wrote to Trobisch it was to say, "I seriously need a partner in my life."[72] Trobisch gave him the advice he gave to so many others: "Pray regularly (daily) that God may show the girl whom he prepared for you and who will be your wife."[73] Trobisch closed his letter with a verse from Psalm 37: "Take delight in the Lord, and he will give you the desires of your heart." When Klu next wrote, he used this verse to tell Trobisch his good news: "I GOT WHAT MY HEART DESIRES. . . . I fell in love with a Girl or rather we both fell in love simultaneously. If really she is the girl God prepared for me I shall very very be thankful to Him."[74] A few months later, however, the woman's father put an end to the relationship. Klu told Trobisch that his faith was sustaining him: "I am happy and this is my astonishment though it troubled me for sometime past but now I'm happy because I feel God's good earth and the world is still beautiful."[75] Throughout the next two years, Klu continued to write to Trobisch as he waited for God to guide him to a wife. When his parents began pressuring him to marry, he told them he could "never marry a girl I don't really know . . . I can't cheat any girl by accepting a marriage planned by someone else."[76] Trobisch commended him for postponing marriage until he found the right woman, and Klu thanked Trobisch "for guiding me not to have picked on a girl which would not have been the chosen one for me from God."[77] Klu then offered a testimony of how God was sustaining him while he waited for the right woman:

> Even right now I am at a cross road with nobody in my mind, I am happy for knowing the Lord Jesus Christ who is so kind to me and has shown it in many diverse ways. I am sure the Lord will do His will for me and I am still waiting for Him anywhere, anytime. One thing I have noticed recently is that I have been so preoccupied and happy in the Lord so much that I have almost forgotten about my bachelorhood. This is not hallucination. The Lord is making it easy for me to go through all these months past and those to come with comfort and free mind.

72. R. Klu to W. Trobisch, 29 April 1976, Walter Trobisch Collection, Box 14, Folder K.
73. W. Trobisch to R. Klu, 29 June 1976, Walter Trobisch Collection, Box 14, Folder K.
74. R. Klu to W. Trobisch, 29 October 1976, Walter Trobisch Collection, Box 14, Folder K.
75. R. Klu to W. Trobisch, 24 February 1977, Walter Trobisch Collection, Box 14, Folder K.
76. R. Klu to W. Trobisch, 13 June 1977, Walter Trobisch Collection, Box 14, Folder K.
77. W. Trobisch to R. Klu, 13 June 1977, and R. Klu to W. Trobisch, 14 December 1978, Walter Trobisch Collection, Box 14, Folder K.

Klu's testimony illustrates the way in which Christian faith could sustain a young person while he waited to find the right woman to marry. Young people like him wrote to Trobisch with questions about how to find and choose a spouse and how to deal with relational disappointments. Their letters thanked Trobisch for guiding them to their faith as a reservoir for approaching their relational quandaries. These young people found prayer extremely helpful in the context of dating because it enabled them to see God as the one ultimately responsible for guiding them through the dating process.

4

Leaders in a Christian Home Movement in Africa

The success of J'ai Aimé Une Fille and the growing correspondence ministry of Marriage Guidance Service for Africa established the Trobisches as leaders in a Christian home movement in Africa. This movement was a joint project of Western missionaries and African Christians, which had been developing since the 1930s. Whereas previous missionaries had always condemned polygamy and the bride-price, Africans and missionaries in the mid-twentieth century began to articulate more nuanced positions on polygamy and the bride-price. They also encouraged churches to hold marriage and family life seminars in order to counter the ill effects of modernization on African family life. In the early-to-mid-1960s, the Trobisches were instrumental in garnering ecumenical support for this marriage guidance movement. They shaped the theological conversation about marriage in Africa through their seminars and books and through Walter's articles, presentations, and radio broadcasts. However, by the 1970s, African theologians and churches were leading the conversation about the Christian home in Africa.

THE ALL-AFRICA LUTHERAN CONFERENCE IN ADDIS ABABA

In October of 1965, Walter Trobisch attended the All-Africa Lutheran Conference in Addis Ababa, where he shared about his marriage counseling ministry by mail. In typical Walter fashion, he issued several provocative and memorable statements at the conference. Firstly, he challenged the church's position on polygamy:

> Maybe our mistake is that we want to establish a general law for all cases. We want to be like God, knowing what is good and evil, and have decided that monogamy is "good" and polygamy "evil" while the word of God clearly does not say so. The Old Testament has no outspoken commandment against polygamy and the New Testament is conspicuously silent about it. Instead of dealing with polygamy, the Bible has a message for polygamists.[1]

In other words, Trobisch was concerned with bringing individual people to Christ, even if those individuals were part of polygamist marriages. Ultimately, Trobisch did believe monogamy was preferable to polygamy. He told a colleague two years earlier that he could "not well imagine a Christian marriage in the deepest sense of the word as a polygamist marriage."[2] And in 1967 he would chastise the Lutheran Church in Liberia for failing to communicate to people that polygamy was sinful.[3] At Addis Ababa in 1965, however, Trobisch wanted to stretch the church to be more flexible in its position on polygamy. He had written to a friend that he believed it was necessary to "deal with every single case separately" instead of dealing with polygamy "in a general way."[4] He had said that the church should "discern between moral and unmoral polygamy as well as between moral and unmoral monogamy." This was essentially the message he offered at Addis Ababa, and it was a fairly progressive message for the time.

Trobisch also stressed the moral ambiguity of the church's position on polygamy. "Our dilemma is that we want monogamy and we do not want divorce. Yet we cannot have one without the other."[5] Ultimately, Trobisch argued that there was a great need for pastoral soul-counseling in African congregations. His catchy statement, "What is needed in Africa are not church disciplinarians, but marriage counselors" was quickly picked up by *Religious News Service* and forwarded around the world.[6] The emperor of Ethiopia, Haile Selassi I, even "heard reports of [Trobisch's] lecture over the

---

1. Trobisch, "Congregational Responsibility for the Christian Individual," 103.
2. W. Trobisch to Paul Hansen, 14 December 1963, Ingrid Trobisch Papers.
3. W. Trobisch, "Report about two Pastors' Refresher Courses held in Addis Ababa and Monrovia, October–December 1967," Ingrid Trobisch Papers.
4. W. Trobisch to Paul Hansen, 14 December 1963, Ingrid Trobisch Papers.
5. Trobisch, "Congregational Responsibility for the Christian Individual," 105.
6. "Pastoral Counseling Held Great Need in Africa."

radio [and] called the station personally expressing his interest and desire that this work of marriage counseling for Africans be continued."[7]

Trobisch's experience at Addis Ababa confirmed his growing conviction that marriage counseling, with the aim of leading people to a closer relationship with God, was his life's calling. Therefore, in the summer of 1966, Walter and Ingrid Trobisch took what they considered a giant step of faith. Rather than returning to Africa as missionaries of the American Lutheran Church, they took "an extended leave of absence without salary."[8] Their furlough salary had supported them from 1963 to 1964 and a couple of scholarships had funded Walter's studies at the University of Heidelberg from 1964 to 1966, but in June of 1966 they began to live simply off the income from their books.[9] They stretched this income to fund both living expenses and the growing ministry of Marriage Guidance Service for Africa (MGSA).

Walter's experience at Addis Ababa also communicated to him that the church at large, specifically the Lutheran Church in Africa, felt that marriage guidance in Africa was a pressing need and that the Trobisches' MGSA was doing a commendable job of meeting that need. This gave him and Ingrid the confidence they needed to step out in faith and live without a guaranteed salary.

TAMBARAM AND THE EAST AFRICAN REVIVAL

When Walter Trobisch challenged the church's position on polygamy at the conference in Addis Ababa in 1965, he had no idea that he was asking questions that African Christians had asked all the way back in 1938 at the meeting of the International Missionary Council (IMC) in Tambaram. Tambaram was the first IMC conference "in which a significant number of Africans took part."[10] At the conference, the fifteen African delegates initiated conversations about polygamy and the appropriateness of related church policies, such as denying communion to people in polygamous marriages. It appears that at least some of the delegates did not think polygamy was inherently antithetical to Christian faith and wanted the church to begin admitting people in polygamous marriages to communion.

---

7. W. and I. Trobisch, "Marriage Guidance Serving Africa," July 1966, Missionary Personnel Files.

8. W. and I. Trobisch, "Marriage Guidance Serving Africa," July 1966, Missionary Personnel Files.

9. "Report of Activities" in W. and I. Trobisch to Dr. Morris Sorenson, 23 August 1971, Missionary Personnel Files.

10. Ludwig, "Tambaram," 49.

Tambaram gave these delegates a chance to bring the church's policy on polygamy to the attention of the international missionary community.[11] In the decades after Tambaram, the IMC researched and published a *Survey of African Marriage and Family Life*, which became an important reference book for missionaries and African church leaders.[12]

Meanwhile, reflection on Christian marriage was also becoming a key component of a revival that swept through East Africa during the 1930s, 1940s, and 1950s. People associated with the East African Revival were called *Balokole* ("saved ones"). The *Balokole* stressed the importance of harmony in the home. Husbands and wives were encouraged to talk about their problems with one another, to resolve conflict before it erupted into greater conflict, and to forgive one another so as to restore the peace in the home. Rather than rejecting the bride-price, as most mission churches in Africa had done, the *Balokole* sought to mediate the aspects of the bride-price that had become oppressive. And rather than rejecting arranged marriage out of hand, the *Balokole* encouraged young people to marry within the "New Clan" of fellow Balokole. Members of the clan, therefore, took it upon themselves to help young people find suitable mates, negotiate marital arrangements with the prospective families, and even acquire the funds for the bride-price.[13]

When the All Africa Conference of Churches (AACC) held its first meeting in Ibadan, Nigeria in 1958, the influence of the East African Revival was clear. Obadiah Kariuki, a "staunch revivalist," gave the first address of the conference, and he took as his topic "Christian Home Life."[14] In his address, Kariuki first described "Christian Home Life as It Ought to Be." He referred to Christ's death as the highest bride-price that had ever been paid and urged husbands to love their wives in a similar manner. He argued that husbands and wives should "work together to make their home a center of peace and joy and love."[15]

Kariuki's address was a way of sharing with delegates from other parts of Africa the kinds of conversations that had been transpiring in East Africa as a result of the East African Revival. It was an invitation for Africans from other geographical regions to pick up the torch and carry the discussion on African marriage forward. The delegates at Ibadan accepted the invitation. When they drew up their report on Home and Family Life, they included

11. Erlank, "Strange Bedfellows," 277.
12. Phillips, *Survey of African Marriage and Family Life*, 1953.
13. Larsson, "Haya Women's Response," 122–23.
14. Karanja, "Confession and Cultural Dynamism," 221.
15. Kariuki, "Christian Home Life," 18–19.

further issues the church should address, for example, the sexual taboo during lactation. The delegates felt this practice should be discouraged because it was "contrary to Scripture," it "leads to wide-spread promiscuity on the part of the husband, and is a major instrument used to justify polygamy."[16] The delegates affirmed Kariuki's demand for marriage counseling and also recommended that the Church "teach, clearly and repeatedly, that Christian marriage involves full co-operation between husband and wife in the financial support and management of the home."[17]

Thus, when the Trobisches began discussing the sexual taboo during lactation during their first missionary term in Cameroon and when they began teaching the marriage course at Libamba during their second term, they were stepping into a much larger conversation than they realized at the time.

LEADERS IN A GROWING CHRISTIAN HOME MOVEMENT

The discussion of Christian marriage and family life, which had been initiated by African delegates to Tambaram in 1938, reached a climax in the 1960s and 70s. The Trobisches became important voices in the movement at that point.

In the early 1960s, Walter Trobisch published several articles on African Christian marriage.[18] As mentioned in chapter 2, he was also invited to serve as chaplain at the All Africa Seminar on the Christian Home in Kitwe, Zambia in 1963. In a bold move, the delegates at Kitwe recommended that if a man in a polygamous marriage converted to Christianity, he should still be granted communion, along with his wives and children.[19] Regarding the bride-price, delegates recommended "that the system be not condemned in itself because of its acknowledged abuse . . . [but rather] that the traditional exchanges be 'Christianized' into a token of the covenant between the partners and their families." Trobisch, himself, was more critical of the bride-price, but his work at Libamba and the publication of *J'ai Aimé Une Fille* helped stimulate the debate about the bride-price that took place at Kitwe. And after Kitwe, Trobisch also helped stimulate conversation about the

---

16. "Reports of Group I," 27.
17. "Reports of Group I," 29.
18. Trobisch, "Church Discipline in Africa"; Trobisch, "Pre-Marital Relations"; Trobisch, "Attitudes of Some African Youth toward Sex and Marriage."
19. All-Africa Seminar on the Christian Home and Family Life, *All-Africa Seminar*, 56.

Christian home among Lutherans at the 1965 conference in Addis Ababa mentioned at the beginning of this chapter.

Trobisch's Position with the Lutheran World Federation

Walter Trobisch made quite a splash at Addis Ababa, and three years later the Lutheran World Federation (LWF) invited him to serve as Consultant on Family Counseling to the churches in Africa.[20] Trobisch's contract with the LWF required him to make two trips to Africa per year and to give a weekly address on Radio Voice of the Gospel, a Christian radio program based out of Addis Ababa. The LWF considered Trobisch's position a two-year "pilot project," but he ended up holding the position for three years. The position with the LWF was a good fit for Trobisch. It funded his trips to Africa and facilitated the contacts he was able to make in Africa. It also enhanced Trobisch's status as a marriage counselor and, through contacts at the LWF and the World Council of Churches, opened up doors for him to present in countries outside of Africa.

Marriage Guidance Service for Africa

Since Trobisch was only employed part-time for the LWF, he spent the rest of his time directing the work of Marriage Guidance Service for Africa (MGSA), the organization the Trobisches and their African protégés, Jean and Ernestine Banyolak, had founded in 1965. The Trobisches, Banyolaks, and the volunteers who assisted them in the work of MGSA believed that their work was on the cutting edge of missionary work in Africa. They wasted no time in promoting their work within Lutheran circles and ecumenical circles in Africa. The same year Trobisch gave a paper at the All-Africa Lutheran conference in Addis Ababa, Jean Banyolak wrote an article for the *All Africa Conference of Churches Bulletin* titled "Africa Needs Marriage Counsellors." In it he proclaimed, "Marriage counseling has a tremendous evangelistic opportunity. It may be the most vital contribution African Churches have to make to the life of their nations and at the same time a most promising door for the Gospel to advance."[21] In 1966, the Trobisches wrote a letter to friends who had supported their work in the past, presenting their plans for the work of MGSA and concluding with what sounded like the mission statement of their organization: "For us marriage guidance is not an end in

---

20. "Africa Family Counseling Consultant is Appointed."
21. Banyolak, "Africa Needs Marriage Counsellors," 69.

itself, but a door for the Gospel of Jesus Christ. We believe that in Africa it is a very promising door. It is our goal and our task to use it."[22]

The Trobisches and Banyolaks conceived of MGSA as having essentially two goals. First, there was the goal of giving marriage guidance through answering the letters that arrived on Trobisch's doorstep. The Trobisches and Banyolaks knew this "marriage guidance by mail" was only a "preliminary 'service,' a help, a substitute until a better solution can be found."[23] The long-term goal of MGSA was to train African pastors, teachers, and doctors in marriage guidance. In order to do this, MGSA proposed developing "correspondence courses on the topic of marriage and the family," holding "regional workshops and seminars in different African countries," writing literature for these seminars, and training African teachers to help lead the seminars. Jean and Ernestine Banyolak were the first such African leaders being trained for the work. Jean had come to Germany with the Trobisches in 1963 and had attended the Institute for Protestant Marriage Counsellors in Berlin. Ernestine had come later and was enrolled in a "course in kindergarten training, home economics and nursing care."[24] Despite the professional, Western training of the couple, the Trobisches were sure to tell their friends that the purpose of MGSA was not "to create in Africa the new profession of a marriage counselor. The immediate goal should be rather to enable those who are already in touch with people (pastors, teachers, doctors, etc.) to give first-aid in marriage problems."[25]

Investigating Clitoridectomy

One of the African marital issues that Walter Trobisch chose to investigate during the 1960s was clitoridectomy and its effects on women's sexual fulfillment. Clitoridectomy is "the partial or complete amputation of the clitoris. It is one of three variants of Female Genital Mutilation," a procedure that is sometimes described as "female circumcision."[26] Clitoridectomy has been practiced "for nearly 2500 years" in regions all around the globe.[27] During

22. W. and I. Trobisch, "Marriage Guidance Serving Africa," July 1966, Missionary Personnel Files.

23. W. and I. Trobisch, "Marriage Guidance Serving Africa," July 1966, Missionary Personnel Files.

24. W. and I. Trobisch, "Marriage Guidance Serving Africa," July 1966, Missionary Personnel Files.

25. W. and I. Trobisch, "Marriage Guidance Serving Africa," July 1966, Missionary Personnel Files.

26. Finzsch and Hulverscheidt, "Cliteridectomy," 1.

27. Slack, "Female Circumcision," 439.

the mid-twentieth century, however, it was most prevalent in East Africa. "Nine out of ten females in Somalia and Sudan" were circumcised.[28] Like other Christians, the Trobisches opposed the practice.

The issue of clitoridectomy and female sexual response was brought to Trobisch's attention at the conference in Addis Ababa in 1965. Many of the men who came to see him for private consultations during the conference complained that their wives had no feeling during sexual intercourse. Since he had not heard of the same complaint in West Africa, Trobisch developed a theory that lack of sexual response in African women was related to the practice of female circumcision. He began to wonder, "Can a woman without a clitoris still arrive at a vaginal orgasm?"[29] When Trobisch found out about the work of Dr. Kegel, who claimed to have found a way of improving female sexual response by strengthening the pubococcygeus muscle, he enlisted Dr. Kegel's advice about clitoridectomy.[30]

Trobisch also spoke with numerous women about the relationship between clitoridectomy and their perceptions of womanhood. He found that the original purpose of clitoridectomy was "a means of emancipation, necessary for self-respect and maturity, the condition sine qua non for full womanhood."[31] However, because it inhibited women sexually and modern men expected their wives to be able to achieve orgasm, the clitoridectomized woman found herself "in a psychological dilemma: Without the operation she does not feel 'clean' and desirable; with the operation she experiences that she is not desirable either, because of her unsatisfactory sexual response. The very operation which was supposed to make her feel mature now makes her feel immature."[32] Trobisch never published his work on clitoridectomy. However, he did incorporate it into the seminars he and Ingrid gave in Africa. To facilitate their discussion about male and female sexual response, they showed slides of the pubococcygeus muscle and talked about the exercises Dr. Kegel had developed. They hoped these "Kegel" exercises might help clitoridectomized women to achieve orgasm by strengthening their pelvic floor.

28. Slack, "Female Circumcision," 443.
29. Trobisch, "Clitoridectomy," 27.
30. Arnold H. Kegel to W. Trobisch, 2 February 1966, Walter Trobisch Collection, Box 13, Folder 16: Clitoridectomy Papers.
31. Trobisch, "Clitoridectomy," 25.
32. Trobisch, "Clitoridectomy," 25.

The "Here is My Problem" Book Series

Between 1965 and 1970, Walter Trobisch and Jean Banyolak addressed other marital issues in a five-book series called "Here is My Problem." Each booklet contained back-and-forth correspondence around a particular topic. In the first booklet, "My Wife Made Me a Polygamist," Trobisch argued that even though the church had an "illogical, contradictory and arbitrary" stance on polygamy, monogamy was still the most desirable form of marriage. In the second booklet, "My Wife has Lost Interest in Sex," Banyolak reproduced and addressed some of the questions about sex, which he had received from Africans. In the third booklet, "My Parents have Become Impossible," Trobisch argued that the lack of communication between the generations was one of Africa's most pressing concerns. In the fourth booklet, "The Person I Married Does Not Obey Me," Trobisch unpacked how many marital troubles could be improved by using the sympto-thermal method of conception control. The fifth booklet, "Can Sex Hurt Love?" contained a number of meditations on the fact that "love is a feeling to be learned" and premarital sex is not a true expression of love.[33] The Trobisches published the five booklets through their own publishing house, Editions Trobisch, and distributed them throughout Africa.[34]

As Trobisch and Banyolak wrote the "Here is My Problem" series, they incorporated many of the opinions and conclusions reached at Kitwe and Ibadan (meetings of the All Africa Conference of Churches). Like Kitwe and Ibadan, the "Here is My Problem" series discussed birth control and advocated equality between spouses. It endorsed monogamy as the ideal but also suggested a more moderate approach to polygamy. Whether Trobisch and Banyolak consciously incorporated Kitwe and Ibadan material into their "Here is My Problem" series is doubtful. Still, it is likely that Trobisch's experience at Kitwe and his knowledge of Ibadan helped to frame the message he conveyed in each booklet.

---

33. "Love is a Feeling to be Learned" was the title of the address Trobisch delivered in 1967 at youth rallies in Seattle, Dallas, Addis Ababa, and Monrovia. The booklet, "Can Sex Hurt Love" contained this address in full, as well as the reproduction of Trobisch's conversation with a girl named Karin, who had further questions about premarital sex.

34. They had founded Editions Trobisch in 1964 with their friend Volker Gscheidle, who became the business manager of the venture. The goal of Editions Trobisch was "to publish and distribute books with a biblical message about marriage and family in English and French in the countries of the Third World" (W. Trobisch, "The Story of Family Life Mission," July 1979, Ingrid Trobisch Papers).

Promoting Natural Family Planning

While Walter was working on the "Here is My Problem" book series, Ingrid also began working on a series of five booklets, which explained elements of the female life cycle from a female perspective.[35] She and Walter envisioned the booklets being read by African husbands in order to better understand their wives. The series, which she called "Understanding Your Wife," was essentially a summary of the lectures she gave in their family life seminars, lectures that drew from her early interactions with the women in Tchollire and from her continuing research on women's reproductive health.

Much of her research in the late 1960s was geared towards finding a more reliable method of natural birth control than that of the rhythm method. Even though condoms were available at the time, they were not readily available in rural Africa. Moreover, Ingrid had found that many Africans had an aversion to condoms and many African governments at the time outlawed artificial contraception.[36]

In 1968, the Trobisches read an article in an Austrian medical journal that caught their attention. It was written by Dr. Josef Roetzer, who had spent twenty years researching women's cycles and who, as it turned out, "lived only a few miles from our home."[37] The Trobisches quickly got in touch with Dr. Roetzer to learn more about the sympto-thermal method of Natural Family Planning (NFP), which he proposed.[38] When they discovered that this method was far more reliable that the rhythm method, they wasted no time in publicizing it in Africa. Walter wrote about it in one of his "Here is My Problem" booklets. He also spoke about NFP in his radio program for Radio Voice of the Gospel, which broadcast from Addis Ababa, Ethiopia.[39] Ingrid lectured about NFP at their next family life seminar in South Africa in May of 1969 and incorporated the information into her book series.[40] She also began attending international conferences, which might educate her or allow her to educate others about NFP. In 1971, she attended the Third

---

35. She wrote the first two of these booklets in 1969. The five booklets were on a woman's cycle, a woman's sexual response, pregnancy, childbirth, and breastfeeding ("Report of Activities" in W. and I. Trobisch to Dr. Morris Sorenson, 23 August 1971, Missionary Personnel Files).

36. Trobisch, *Joy of Being a Woman*, 42.

37. Trobisch, *Joy of Being a Woman*, 42.

38. The Sympto-Thermal Method taught a woman how to determine her fertility by taking her basal body temperature, observing her cervical mucus and the position of her cervix, and observing other bodily markers of fertility like pain in her uterus and tender breasts (Roetzer, "Sympto-Thermal Method").

39. "Biographical Profile," Human Life Foundation, Ingrid Trobisch Papers.

40. "Report of South African Trip—May, 1969," Walter Trobisch Collection, Box 19.

International Congress of Psychosomatic Obstetrics and Gynecology, and she lectured on NFP at the group's next conference three years later.[41]

The Trobisches' Marriage Seminars: Presenting as a Couple to Couples

Although only Walter was officially employed by the LWF, as often as she could, Ingrid arranged for someone to care for the children so that she could accompany Walter and present by his side. The Trobisches believed "that the most effective way to teach a marriage course is by a couple to couples."[42] Not only was it more enjoyable for them to present as a couple, but they also believed presenting as a couple demonstrated their message about gender roles in a very concrete way: "If we want to dethrone patriarchalism in Africa, and at the same time make marriage guidance a matter where a man talks exclusively to men, we defeat our own purpose."[43]

Some of the Trobisches' seminars lasted only one week and others lasted three to four weeks. Participants would usually attend a couple of class sessions each morning, with an afternoon reserved for reading, recreation, and individual consultations with Walter. The Trobisches often arranged for a library to be prepared in advance at the seminar site with books that would complement their lectures.

The Trobisches' message on marriage centered on one verse in the Bible: "Therefore shall a man leave his father and his mother, and shall cleave unto his wife: and they shall be one flesh."[44] The Trobisches elaborated on each element of this verse. They called "leaving" the legal, public declaration of marriage and described how necessary it was for the new couple to make a clean break from their kin. They described "cleaving" as the personal, emotional side of marriage and "becoming one flesh" as the physical side of marriage. They stressed how important it was for a couple to "share everything they have, not only their bodies, not only their material possessions, but also their thinking and their feeling, their joy and their suffering, their hopes and their fears, their successes and their failures."[45] The Trobisches also drew attention to the fact that children were not mentioned in Genesis 2:24, which meant

---

41. W. and I. Trobisch to friends, October 1974, Ingrid Trobisch Papers.
42. W. and I. Trobisch to friends, November 1968, Ingrid Trobisch Papers.
43. W. and I. Trobisch to friends, November 1969, Ingrid Trobisch Papers.
44. Gen 2:24, KJV.
45. Trobisch, *Complete Works of Walter Trobisch*, 383.

that children were not a necessary but rather an enhancing part of marriage. Children were "an additional blessing."⁴⁶

When giving marriage seminars, Walter would often draw a triangle on the board to represent what he called "the biblical concept of marriage." In the angles of the triangle he would write "leaving," "cleaving," and "one flesh." He would then talk about how "the biblical concept of marriage" contradicted "the garden concept of marriage," which was prevalent in much of the world. He had gotten "the garden concept of marriage" from reading *Marriage East and West,* a book by marriage counselors David and Vera Mace. "The garden concept of marriage," he said, "conceives of the man as the sower of the seed and of the woman as the soil . . . Man plants his seed in the woman. The woman's body nurtures the seed as the soil nurtures the grain of rice. Just as the plant grows out of the grain, so the child grows out of the man's seed."⁴⁷ According to the Maces and the Trobisches, there were many problems with "the garden concept of marriage." In short, it propagated a misunderstanding of biology, the inequality of the sexes, the brideprice, polygamy, and divorce. Furthermore, it depicted unmarried people and childless marriages as pointless. "The biblical concept of marriage," on the other hand, fit well with an accurate understanding of biology and supported monogamy and the equality of the sexes.

While leading seminars in Africa the Trobisches also addressed other elements of family life besides marriage. In a report on one trip to Africa, Walter wrote that he covered "difference in male and female sexual response; biology of fertilization; pregnancy and birth; conception control; circumcision and clitoridectomy, [and] sex education of children."⁴⁸ To facilitate the discussion on birth, they occasionally showed *Naissance,* a film prepared by Dr. Pierre Vellay, who was Dr. Lamaze's assistant.⁴⁹ The film not only highlighted the natural method of childbirth, which the Trobisches advocated, but it also showed how the father could take an active role in childbirth.⁵⁰ In their discussion about birth control the Trobisches always imparted the latest information about natural family planning, their preferred method of birth control.

The Trobisches often had the sense that what they were doing was something completely new. They got that impression when they gave seminars

46. Trobisch, *I Married You,* 25–26.
47. Trobisch, *Complete Works of Walter Trobisch,* 387.
48. W. Trobisch, "Report about two Pastors' Refresher Courses held in Addis Ababa and Monrovia, October–December 1967," Ingrid Trobisch Papers.
49. Zwelling, "History of Lamaze Continues."
50. W. and I. Trobisch to friends, February 1976, Ingrid Trobisch Papers.

and found that there were not words in the indigenous language to describe the concepts they were discussing. During a seminar in Addis Ababa, Walter discovered that the pastors did not know "the biology of fertilization." He wrote in his report of the event, "It became so evident to the class that simple biological information could have prevented many a case of adultery, divorce and even polygamy"[51] The Trobisches also got a sense of the novelty of their work when participants repeatedly stressed their surprise about "the fact that 'God and sex had something to do with each other'" and when participants were shocked to hear Ingrid, a woman, discussing sex and childbirth to a public audience of both men and women.[52] As Josiah Kibira, a bishop in the Evangelical Lutheran Church of Tanzania, told Walter after the Trobisches gave a seminar in his diocese, "Could you please pass my very sincere love to your wife whose service to us will be remembered for the whole future of our Pastor's services. Yours also, of course, but they have heard men teachers and not so many women clever and loving lecturers as your wife."[53] The Trobisches also realized the pressing need for their work when African pastors lamented the lack of suitable literature for leading seminars on Christian family life with their congregations.[54]

In leading seminars and composing literature on a Christian view of sex, marriage, and family, the Trobisches felt they were doing important work and answering a need in African churches. The positive response they received in letters and seminars confirmed their feeling. After Walter's seminar in Liberia, Bishop Roland Payne went so far as to argue that the LWF should "set up a department on marriage counseling to be headed by Pastor Walter Trobisch."[55]

THE TOLL ON THE CHILDREN

Walter and Ingrid Trobisch felt assured that what they were doing was important, but their work took a toll on their children. To the Trobisch children, it seemed that their parents were always just getting back from a trip or about to leave. Stephen remarked later that when he was a child, "It was one

51. W. Trobisch, "Report about two Pastors' Refresher Courses held in Addis Ababa and Monrovia, October–December 1967," Ingrid Trobisch Papers.

52. Trobisch, *My Journey Homeward*, 86; W. and I. Trobisch to friends, November 1969, Ingrid Trobisch Papers.

53. Josiah Kibira to W. Trobisch, 23 December 1971, Walter Trobisch Collection, Box 6.

54. Gebremedhin, "Nurture of the People of God," 68.

55. Dr. Roland Payne to Dr. Christian Walther, 13 December 1967, Walter Trobisch Collection, Box 19.

of the hardest things for me to see [Father] and Mother leave.... I can well remember how [Father] asked me once what would make me happy. I said, 'The coming back home.'" Walter's response was not exactly comforting: "How can you come back home if you have not been away from home?"[56] The Trobisches did feel bad about leaving the children and said they "would not dare [to do it] if it were only for adventure's sake."[57] Ingrid also found the preparations for their travels tiring. She had to constantly remind herself, "When God gives us a commission, He also gives us the strength to fulfill it."[58] It was this belief that God had called them to give marriage guidance in Africa that made the Trobisches press on, despite the exhaustion it caused and the negative effects it had on their children. The Trobisches interpreted the many "open doors" for their message as confirmation of God's call. Further confirmation came each time they gave a message and felt energized by it. As Walter wrote after speaking in Liberia at the end of 1967, "I was filled with deep joy—a joy that can only be felt when you do the work God gives you and stand at the place God puts you."[59]

Still, although they loved their work, they decided in the summer of 1968 to forgo their mission plans and simply spend time with their children. Back in February of 1968, the All Africa Conference of Churches had invited Walter to lead a Family Life seminar for French-speaking West Africa.[60] Walter had accepted the invitation, but when he and Ingrid decided it would be better to be "family egoists," he canceled the invitation. As the Trobisches wrote in their newsletter, "We felt that we had no authority to give messages on family life if we neglect our own."[61]

PASSING THE TORCH

During the 1960s, the Trobisches were leaders in the Christian home movement in Africa. They popularized the movement and shaped the theological discussion about Christian family life through their marriage seminars, radio programs, books, and correspondence ministry Marriage Guidance Service for Africa. At least among ecumenical Protestants and evangelicals, the Trobisches' theology of the Christian home, as expressed at Kitwe in

56. Trobisch, *My Journey Homeward*, 114.
57. W. and I. Trobisch to friends, November 1969, Ingrid Trobisch Papers.
58. W. and I. Trobisch to friends, June 1970, Missionary Personnel Files.
59. Trobisch, *My Journey Homeward*, 72.
60. Melle Cox van Heemstra to Chers Frères et Soeurs en Christ, Février 1968, Walter Trobisch Collection, Box 21, Folder 36.
61. W. and I. Trobisch to friends, November 1968, Ingrid Trobisch Papers.

1963, the All-Africa Lutheran Conference of 1965, and in their various seminars and publications helped set the stage for African-led theological refection on the Christian home, which developed in the 1970s.

John Mbiti

African theologian John Mbiti was one of the most significant people to pick up the torch from the Trobisches in the 1970s. Mbiti advocated most of the same sexual ethics that the Trobisches did.[62] However, he made more allowances for African tradition than had previous missionaries and African church leaders. He said arranged marriages showed "the social importance of marriage, especially as it concerns the families and relatives of the couple."[63] In regards to the bride-price, he first chastised missionaries for their decision to call the exchange of marital gifts a bride-price: "The exchange of betrothal and marriage goods and services is not an act of purchase, and most African words for this custom are different from words used for buying and selling goods. It is absolute nonsense to call the exchange bride-price or dowry."[64]

Mbiti expressed a sentiment felt by many Africans. Trobisch had encountered this perspective at Libamba. While teaching his marriage class in 1960, one of his students, Pierre Oko Mengue, had rebuked Trobisch for so adamantly opposing the bride-price without having a deep understanding of its purpose. However, it should also be noted that in that same Libamba marriage class were students who felt, as Trobisch did, that the bride-price tradition had deteriorated into a form of buying and selling. As the heroine in Guillaume Oyono Mbia's play *Trois Prétendants* declared, "Am I to be sold to the highest bidder? Can I not be consulted about my own wedding?"[65] African women had also been calling for the abolition of the bride-price since at least the 1950s.[66] And during that time several studies had found that "the educated African increasingly disapproves of the custom."[67]

Mbiti's perspective on the bride-price was deeply affected by his desire to separate African Christianity from Western influence. Thus even though

---

62. He affirmed premarital chastity, self-selection of spouses, love as essential to marriage, dating, intimacy and equality of husband and wife in marriage, the independence of a married couple from extended kin, and the belief that children are not necessary for marriage.

63. Mbiti, *Love and Marriage in Africa*, 50.

64. Mbiti, *Love and Marriage in Africa*, 63.

65. Mbia, *Trois Prétendants*, 17–18.

66. Marie André du Sacré Cœur, *House Stands Firm*, 229–31.

67. Goode, *World Revolution and Family Patterns*, 177.

there were many Africans who saw more negatives than positives in the continued use of the bride-price, Mbiti chose to associate that perspective with Western missionaries and to stress the positives of the bride-price system. Using the theologically-charged word, covenant, Mbiti called the betrothal gifts "symbols of the marriage covenant." He argued that betrothal and marriage gifts helped to convey the idea that "marriage is a process rather than an event which takes place on the wedding day. It is a process which starts with betrothal or even courtship . . . and . . . may not end until, in some societies, the wife has given birth to one or more children." Mbiti argued that there was no reason that the Western view of marriage as an event sanctioned on one day in the church had to be the way African Christians viewed marriage. He believed the exchange of gifts had "a great value and meaning socially, emotionally, symbolically, morally and economically."[68] In 1963, delegates at the AACC seminar on Christian home and family life at Kitwe had called for the "Christianization" of the bride-price. Mbiti's explanation of the bride-price was the first developed attempt to do just that. He advised young men to embrace the tradition of the bride-price and to give their fiancé's family "as much service as your time will allow you—it is one way of showing that you value the relationship which is being established; and it will also give you an opportunity to understand her and her people better, and for them to understand you and your people better."[69]

Mbiti's more open stance toward African marital customs was also evident in his attitude toward polygamy. Like Walter Trobisch and the delegates at Kitwe, Mbiti distinguished between the institution of polygamy and individual polygamists.[70] He saw "polygamy as becoming increasingly unworkable, outdated and a social deficit." Nevertheless, he affirmed the practice "in the context in which it has evolved and become a normal way of life in our traditional setting."[71] He therefore criticized missionaries for making polygamy a "test of churchmanship," for forcing polygamist converts to divorce all but one wife.[72] Like the delegates at Kitwe, he argued that polygamists should be accepted into the church, even if the church continued to preach monogamy as the ideal.

Mbiti's acceptance of polygamy went even further than Kitwe, however, in that he did not condemn polygamy as a sin for Christians after conversion to Christianity. He said that the church should bless the marriage

68. Mbiti, *Love and Marriage in Africa*, 64.
69. Mbiti, *Love and Marriage in Africa*, 64–65.
70. Mbiti, *Love and Marriage in Africa*, 191.
71. Mbiti, *Love and Marriage in Africa*, 82.
72. Mbiti, *Love and Marriage in Africa*, 189.

of a man with a barren wife to another woman, if the first wife agreed to the marriage.[73] He also thought the church should allow a man who worked far from home to have "one wife looking after the family on the land, while the other is with him in the distant town or city where he works." Such an arrangement, he argued, was "a very plausible, practical and understandable way of facing the situation of life honestly and fairly. It is more sensible and moral than chasing after prostitutes."[74]

Mbiti's openness to polygamy was not shared by the Trobisches. The Trobisches wanted the church to welcome polygamist *converts*, but they did not want future generations of Christians to continue to be practicing polygamy. They saw polygamy as oppressive to women.

The Circle of Concerned African Women Theologians

The Trobisches' perspective on polygamy was shared by African women theologians, who increasingly contributed to the theological conversation about the Christian home during the 1980s. At the inaugural meeting of the Circle of Concerned African Women Theologians, Catholic Sister Anne Nasimiyu-Wasike expressed an opinion shared by most members of the Circle when she argued that polygamy "exploits women for the benefit of men."[75]

Nasimiyu-Wasike and the other African women theologians rejected the idea that affirming polygamy was a way of affirming the inculturation of the gospel in Africa. "To use polygamy as a criterion for inculturation is to miss the whole point of inculturation."[76] Inculturation, argued Nasimiyu-Wasike, is the process whereby "Christ gives meaning to [one's] culture by purifying, sanctifying, elevating and restoring it to wholeness." Since Christ "denounced whatever enslaved people and rejected anything that kept people from appreciating their basic human dignity," and since "polygamy is one of those systems that legalize the inferiority and subordination of women to men," then a truly enculturated African Christianity would reject polygamy. The attentiveness of the Trobisches to the concerns of African women during the 1950s and 1960s can be seen in some ways as anticipating the feminist aims of *The Circle of Concerned African Women Theologians* in the 1980s.

---

73. Mbiti, *Love and Marriage in Africa*, 192.
74. Mbiti, *Love and Marriage in Africa*, 195.
75. Nasimiyu-Wasike, "Polygamy," 104.
76. Nasimiyu-Wasike, "Polygamy," 115.

Byang Kato

The Trobisches' involvement in the Christian home movement can also be seen as anticipating the work of Byang Kato and other African evangelicals. Kato has been called "the founding father of modern African evangelical theology."[77] He and his wife Jummai were particularly interested in getting evangelicals to have family devotions, which would presumably train up their children in the faith. The Katos "put an emphasis on prayer and Bible reading in their home."[78] They were delighted when all three of their children professed personal Christian faith at a young age.

In 1969, at a gathering of African evangelicals, Kato lectured on "The Youth in the African Church." In this lecture he lamented that "in many Christian homes family worship, joint family devotions, and prayers are not observed," and he argued that "a good Christian home should be the foundation of youth work."[79] Kato's frustration with the failure of African Christians to cultivate truly Christian homes is reminiscent of Trobisch's frustration with American Christians in 1957. Both men became leaders in the Christian home movement in Africa, along with John Mbiti, and Sister Anne Nasimiyu-Wasike. They and others who were active in the movement sought to bring Christianity into conversation with people's everyday lives. Marriage and family life lay at the heart of people's lived experience. To help people understand the teachings of the Christian faith regarding home and family life was a way of deepening people's faith, educating children in the faith, and drawing other people into the faith. Providing theological reflection on African sexual and marital practices was also a way of aiding the process of Christian inculturation in Africa.

THE TERMINATION OF TROBISCH'S CONTRACT WITH THE LUTHERAN WORLD FEDERATION

In the early 1960s, the Trobisches were instrumental in stimulating, shaping, and popularizing the Christian home movement in Africa, but by the late 1960s their importance as leaders in the movement was beginning to fade. Enough African church leaders like Mbiti and Kato had become advocates of marriage guidance that it was no longer necessary for Western missionaries like the Trobisches to be at the forefront of the movement. In postcolonial Africa, continued missionary leadership was not only

---

77. Ferdinando, "Byang Kato, 1936–1975."
78. Breman, *Association of Evangelicals in Africa*, 44.
79. Breman, *Association of Evangelicals in Africa*, 64.

unnecessary but actually in some cases detrimental because it gave credence to the view that Christianity was bound up with colonialism. Recognizing this, the Lutheran World Federation (LWF) notified Trobisch in the fall of 1970 to let him know that his position would be terminated as of December 1971.[80] The LWF had decided that instead of funding a Western marriage counselor, it would set aside a pool of funds from which African churches could draw "for the setting up of seminars around family counseling and for the training of their own personnel for such programs."[81]

The Trobisches did not take the news well; they felt confused, hurt, and angry. They loved their work, they had always received positive feedback, and they still had enough invitations from churches in Africa that they could "easily keep busy until 1975."[82] They spent the rest of 1970 and 1971 trying to make sense of the LWF's decision and to figure out whether another position could be found for them either in the LWF or in another organization.[83] Ultimately, no suitable arrangements could be found, and rather than accept the decision of the LWF, Walter Trobisch continued to fight for the reinstatement of his contract. Josiah Kibira was the person he pressured most heavily.

Correspondence with Josiah Kibira

African bishop Josiah Kibira chaired the LWF commission whose task it was to either renew or terminate Trobisch's contract. Kibira presided as bishop over the North Western Diocese of the Evangelical Lutheran Church in Tanzania. He had given the keynote address at the Lutheran Conference in Addis Ababa in 1965, where Trobisch had done so much to stimulate conversation about African marital issues. Bishop Kibira had been impressed by Trobisch and invited him and Ingrid to give two marriage seminars in Bukoba, Tanzania. They finally did so in October of 1971. While there, Walter Trobisch decided to raise the issue of his contract. It seems that he hoped to find out why Kibira had not defended him at the meeting of the LWF in Tokyo the previous spring and to enlist his help in advocating for the reinstatement of his contract. He told Kibira that several other African church leaders, upon finding that his contract had been terminated, felt "they were deprived of the Service which they want and need."[84] Kibira

80. W. and I. Trobisch to friends, January 1971, Ingrid Trobisch Papers.
81. Carl Hellberg to Morris Sorenson, 16 March 1972, Missionary Personnel Files.
82. W. and I. Trobisch to friends, January 1971, Ingrid Trobisch Papers.
83. For a fuller discussion, see Stasson, "Love, Sex, and Marriage," ch. 5.
84. W. Trobisch to Josiah Kibira, 20 January 1972, Walter Trobisch Collection, Box 6.

apparently showed some concern about the situation, for he wrote "some of [his] thoughts" to Carl Hellberg, another LWF administrator.[85] Kibira also asked Trobisch "to leave the matters to me and let me speak and hear what my own pastors think about your work." Presumably, after he had spoken with other African pastors, Kibira would then have gotten back in touch with Trobisch or would have written another letter to Carl Hellberg or LWF secretary Andre Appel.

Trobisch, however, was impatient. Rather than waiting for Kibira to proceed in the manner he saw fit, Trobisch used his conversation with Kibira to bolster his own position in a letter he sent to secretary Andre Appel on October 26, 1971. Trobisch said to Appel that when he had been at Kibira's house, Kibira had told him that he would not have voted to end Trobisch's contract if he "would have fully grasped the consequences."[86] Whether Kibira fully meant this, whether he was simply trying to commiserate with Trobisch and offer solace in the face of disappointment, whether Trobisch was remembering the conversation incorrectly, or whether Trobisch deliberately misrepresented Kibira is not clear. In any case, Trobisch told Appel that Kibira was in favor of the reinstatement of his contract with the LWF. Appel then showed the letter to Kibira during Kibira's visit to Geneva later that year. Understandably, Kibira felt betrayed. After seeing the letter, he told Trobisch, "I don't agree with the way you have patched up pieces of sentences and phrases from our talks at different moments and make them appear to sound like a sequential discussion."[87] He called Trobisch's letter "malicious" and said it made him seem like "a schizophrenic if not completely absent minded type of person."[88]

Missionary Paternalism

The correspondence between Trobisch and Kibira not only illuminates the way in which Trobisch betrayed Kibira's trust. It also demonstrates the extent to which Trobisch held severely paternalistic attitudes. In comparison with many of their peers during the 1950s and 1960s, the Trobisches had been relatively progressive in their views of mission, their efforts to combat

---

85. Josiah Kibira to W. Trobisch, 25 November 1971, Walter Trobisch Collection, Box 6.
86. W. Trobisch to Josiah Kibira, 20 January 1972, Walter Trobisch Collection, Box 6.
87. Josiah Kibira to W. Trobisch, 25 November 1971, Walter Trobisch Collection, Box 6.
88. Josiah Kibira to W. Trobisch, 25 November 1971, Walter Trobisch Collection, Box 6.

racism, and their sensitivity to African culture. However, Trobisch's inability to accept the decision of the LWF to terminate his contract and his efforts to manipulate Kibira demonstrate the sharp limits of his cultural sensitivity. Because so many Africans had given the Trobisches positive feedback in response to their marriage guidance work, the Trobisches simply could not see the other issues at stake in the decision of the LWF to terminate Trobisch's contract. Rather than take a moment to wonder if the decision might really be in the best interest of Christian mission in Africa, Trobisch tried desperately to get the LWF to reinstate his contract.

In January of 1972, after the heat of previous correspondence had subsided, Trobisch wrote to Kibira in order to explain his actions in a way he thought Kibira would find more acceptable. He told Kibira that one of the reasons he initially wrote the letter to Secretary Andre Appel of the LWF was that he wanted "to protect you. You see, Josiah, you see yourself and your position only in the light of Geneva and of the Commission. But I see you in the light of the African Church Leaders who criticise you because they feel that at Tokyo they were deprived of the Service which they want and need."[89] This desire to "protect" Kibira—who was a bishop of the Lutheran Church in Tanzania—and Trobisch's audacity in claiming to know the African church better than Kibira must have struck Kibira as frustrating, to say the least. And there was more: "From our talks," wrote Trobisch, "I got necessarily the impression that at Tokyo you were manipulated and used for certain goals and theological trends of which you yourself were not fully aware."[90] Through statements like this, Trobisch revealed that his years in Africa had done little to supplant his own deeply rooted paternalism.

Evidence of missionary paternalism is also evident in a letter Trobisch sent four years earlier, congratulating Kibira on the birth of twins. He wrote:

> You suddenly have now a large family and that means also a very large responsibility. I pray that you may be able to take this responsibility before God and that in this way your family may become a silent witness not only of the Lord's grace but also of what it means to be a father and a mother in Christ. There is no other way to teach effectively what Christian marriage means than the example of life. I pray that you may be able to give with your wonderful wife, whom I also know, this testimony in order that through it many troubled families may be helped, not only in your church, but all over Africa.[91]

---

89. W. Trobisch to Josiah Kibira, 20 January 1972, Walter Trobisch Collection, Box 6.
90. W. Trobisch to Josiah Kibira, 20 January 1972, Walter Trobisch Collection, Box 6.
91. W. Trobisch to Josiah Kibira, 27 January 1968, Walter Trobisch Collection, Box 14.

The letter reads as if it were written from a father to his child. Trobisch had no ill intentions in composing it. On the contrary, he truly felt that Kibira and his "wonderful wife" were powerful examples of Christian family life, and he wanted to encourage them in this calling. The problem was that Josiah and Martha Kibira already knew the responsibilities associated with parenthood, as well as the responsibilities of being leaders of the church in Africa. They did not need Trobisch to preach to them about these responsibilities. That he did preach likely suggested to them that he did not as yet fully respect them as his equals in the global church. And it was this persistent attitude of missionary paternalism that African church leaders like Kibira detested.

The Kibiras, like the Trobisches, had long been interested in the missional aspects of marriage. They had been active in the East African Revival. Their own marriage had challenged various aspects of traditional African culture. Josiah Kibira noted, "According to Customary Law I had no right to marry this woman as she was of a royal family and I came from a quite simple fisherman's family. I had myself obtained the consent of my wife."[92] Martha also had "permission from her father to marry a young man whom she would choose." The couple perceived their wedding in 1951 as a testimony of the power of Christ to bring people together despite potential cultural barriers. Their wedding offered further testimony to Christ when Martha proceeded to smile throughout the ceremony instead of crying, as was customary for a bride to do at her wedding.[93] Throughout their married life together the Kibiras cultivated a close and loving relationship centered on Christ.

The Kibira's solid marital partnership—from their initial decision to marry for love to their efforts to cultivate marital intimacy over the course of their life together—was exactly the kind of marriage the Trobisches advocated. Thus on the one hand, Josiah Kibira had reason to support the work the Trobisches were doing. But on the other hand, he had reason to find it superfluousness. That is to say, as long as there were Africans like the Kibiras, for whom Christian faith led them to pursue marriages based on love, intimacy, and partnership and to encourage other Africans to do the same, then there was not a real need for Westerners like the Trobisches to be doing marriage guidance work in Africa. Moreover, people like the Kibiras found themselves fighting a war on two fronts. They defended their Christian faith against the critique leveled against them by some of their

---

92. Quoted in Larsson, "Haya Women's Response," 122.

93. Traditionally, a bride would lament leaving her blood relations, but the *Balokole* believed that their ties to one another transcended the ties of blood relations (Larsson, *Bishop Josiah Kibira*, 111–12).

African peers that Christianity was part and parcel of Western colonialism. At the same time, they knew that Christianity *was* still in some ways bound up with colonial structures, so they confronted these colonial structures and attitudes in the church of the global north and called the church in Africa to break free.[94]

Trobisch had always maintained that his goal was to train African pastors, teachers, and doctors to do marriage guidance themselves. However, it seems that he was not able to accept the fact that the marriage guidance work in Africa might actually be able to continue without him overseeing it. As he wrote in a letter to Kibira after it was clear that his contract with the LWF would not be reinstated, "I only want to inform you that, unless another arrangement is found, the work which has begun in many churches—as it did in your church—will probably come to an end."[95] It did not occur to Trobisch that the work might actually continue, even if he were not a part of it. One reason for this was that he was so invested in it. He and Ingrid had been advocating monogamy and marital partnership since 1953, when they first arrived in Tchollire. Ever since he took the post at Libamba in 1957, they had been developing courses and writing books to help young people in modern, urban Africa stay chaste before marriage and cultivate intimacy within marriage. While Trobisch was employed as the LWF's Consultant on Family Counseling to the churches in Africa, the Trobisches gave numerous family life seminars in different parts of Africa. That their message was necessary and unique was confirmed time and again by their positive reception at seminars, as well as by the rapid spread and popularity of Trobisch's *J'ai Aimé Une Fille*.

Church leaders like Kibira could see things that Trobisch could not. Because Trobisch had experienced first-hand how novel the work had been ten years earlier and because he had derived such pleasure from being an instigator in putting family life on the agenda of the LWF, Trobisch was blind to some of the changes that, by 1970, had made his work less necessary. Trobisch realized that his message about marital intimacy had been accepted by most of the African church's elites.[96] But he didn't see that the very success of his work meant that ten years later it was not as important and relevant. At least within the LWF, family life was not seen as a pressing concern in the same way that it had been pressing and novel in the early 1960s. By 1970, the need to give greater autonomy and

---

94. Kibira, "Living Church in a Changing Society," 19.

95. W. Trobisch to Josiah Kibira, 20 January 1972, Walter Trobisch Collection, Box 6.

96. W. Trobisch to Ezra Gebremedhin, 16 September 1972, Walter Trobisch Collection, Box 4: Trobisch Africa, A-Z 1963–1973, Besondere.

institutional leadership to the "younger" churches was the pressing issue. Because Trobisch was so focused on the individual needs for marriage guidance in various churches in Africa, he could not see that at a national and international level his work was no longer as pressing as it had been earlier in the decade. Moreover, since African church leaders themselves were advocating monogamy and marital partnership, his own continuing determination to do so undercut the very claim he had been making about ultimately wanting to turn the work over to Africans.

FAMILY LIFE MISSION

Persistent missionary paternalism is not the only reason Trobisch fought so hard to have his contract with the LWF reinstated. Several times in his correspondence with Kibira, he made an effort to distinguish between his own "personal situation" and "the continuation of the Family Life Work in Africa."[97] He argued that his deepest reason for fighting for his contract was that he wanted to ensure that the people who had expressed to him such anguished need for marriage guidance would be answered. In the Spring of 1972, he began to see a new way of answering this need. The Mission Director of the American Lutheran Church (ALC) suggested to Trobisch that he found his own organization and essentially expand the work of MGSA.[98] It would then be possible for the ALC to make a financial contribution to their organization. The Trobisches were quick to act on the suggestion. They contacted Lutheran pastors in Bavaria to help them form an organization. They asked Augustana Lutheran Church in Minneapolis to process contributions and issue tax receipts.[99] They changed Walter's clergy status with the ALC to "On Loan" to the Bavarian Lutheran Church and developed a four-person steering committee for their organization.[100] They called their organization Family Life Mission. In brochures they drew up later, they expanded on the significance of each of these three words: "We conceive of this work as MISSION because we believe that the renewal of the FAMILY is possible only through the One Who has said, 'I am the LIFE.'"[101]

Ingrid sent out the Trobisches' next *Rundbrief* in December of 1972. Her letter was full of hope. The future of Family Life Mission (FLM) seemed

97. W. Trobisch to Josiah Kibira, 20 January 1972, Walter Trobisch Collection, Box 6.
98. W. and I. Trobisch to friends, 9 March 1972, Ingrid Trobisch Papers.
99. W. and I. Trobisch to friends, December 1972, Ingrid Trobisch Papers.
100. "The American Lutheran Church Application for Extended Service," 5 July 1972, Missionary Personnel Files.
101. "Family Life Mission," May 1973, Missionary Personnel Files.

secure. The Trobisches expected both the ALC and the Bavarian Lutheran Church to contribute to FLM. Although the ALC did not contribute to FLM that first year, the Bavarian Church Mission Department did contribute "two-thirds of our personal support."[102] In addition, the LCA contributed two thousand dollars, and a number of the Trobisches' personal friends also supported them.[103] In 1973, the Trobisches wrote up a history of FLM and clarified for supporters what their contributions would finance: "Support of the Banyolak family in Douala, Cameroun, Correspondence with readers of our books and listeners to our radio programs . . . [and] travel costs for seminars and lecture tours."[104]

For the rest of the decade, until Walter's sudden death in 1979, the Trobisches carried on the correspondence ministry of FLM from their home in the Austrian Alps and traveled to many parts of the world to give seminars. On one occasion, Ingrid was not able to accompany Walter to give a seminar in Papua New Guinea so the Trobisches' son Daniel went instead. The Trobisches later told friends that when Daniel taught about "fertilization, pregnancy, and birth," the New Guineans "couldn't get over the fact that a young, unmarried man was allowed to know all these 'secrets' and talk about them. And this in the presence of his father!" The Trobisches concluded, "Daniel's testimony said more about sex education than a long lecture on our part would have done."[105]

During their seminars, the Trobisches often continued to find that their work was desperately needed. For example, after participating in the Trobisch seminar in Papua New Guinea, Pastor Eoko gave this glowing report: "Before we participated in the Family Life Seminar in Asoroka in 1975 my wife and I were filled with fear. . . . Even when we joined in sexual union we were filled with fear. . . . During the course in Asoroka in 1975 our eyes were opened for God's way. The fear has passed away and I have become now really one flesh with my wife."[106] Another couple, the Mantaris, had been unable to conceive a child prior to the Trobisch seminar. Afterwards, they gave birth to two children.[107]

---

102. "Family Life Mission," May 1973, Missionary Personnel Files.

103. W. Trobisch to Morris Sorenson, 10 April 1973, Ingrid Trobisch Papers; W. and I. Trobisch to friends, December 1972, Ingrid Trobisch Papers.

104. "Family Life Mission," May 1973, Missionary Personnel Files.

105. W. and I. Trobisch to friends, February 1976, Ingrid Trobisch Papers.

106. "Report on Family Life Work in the Lutheran Church of Papua New Guinea, August 1979," Ingrid Trobisch Papers.

107. "Report on Family Life Work in the Lutheran Church of Papua New Guinea, August 1979," Ingrid Trobisch Papers.

However, on other occasions, the Trobisches misjudged their audience. This was apparent at the 1977 meeting of the Association of Evangelicals of Africa and Madagascar in Ivory Coast. As part of his presentation, Walter Trobisch showed *Naissance,* a graphic film about a woman giving birth. *Naissance* had been a helpful part of the Trobisches' seminar in Papua New Guinea two years earlier, but in Ivory Coast many of the delegates chose to avert their eyes rather than view the film. *Naissance* had stimulated conversation for the couples in Papua New Guinea, but it had the opposite effect on the mostly male attendees in Ivory Coast.[108] Most of these male delegates were already familiar with the basic concepts the Trobisches dealt with in their seminars; some of them were, in fact, highly educated.[109] For them, being shown a graphic film about childbirth by a middle-aged missionary probably felt not only out of place but insulting.

It was shortsighted of Trobisch to fail to tailor his message to his African audience. However, his experience in Ivory Coast also pointed to something he should have been celebrating, namely the fact that marriage guidance had become a central part of the mission of the church in Africa. When the Trobisches had begun their work in the early 1960s, their public, couple-centered articulation of what they called "a positive view" of sex and marriage was fairly unique in the Christian community.[110] Many people in their seminars expressed surprise that "God and sex had something to do with each other" and were pleased to be given information about the biological processes of reproduction.[111] African church leaders were in the initial stages of embracing the importance of marriage guidance for mission. In 1966, the Trobisches had spoken emphatically about marriage guidance as "a door for the Gospel of Jesus Christ." They were not the only people saying this in 1966, but they were certainly among the influential people pressing the vision forward.

By 1977, however, family life was on the agenda, evidenced by the fact that the Ivory Coast conference was devoted to the theme of "The Christian Home." As churches commenced giving premarital counseling, as the AACC's Department on Home and Family Life began coordinating family life work throughout Africa, and as books like John Mbiti's *Love and Marriage in Africa* came out, more and more African Christians were conversant in a nuanced, Christian view of sex and marriage.

---

108. Tiénou, conversation, 16 March 2013.

109. Tite Tiénou went on to become the Dean of Trinity Evangelical Divinity School in Deerfield, Illinois.

110. Trobisch, "Church Discipline in Africa," 202.

111. W. and I. Trobisch to friends, November 1969, Ingrid Trobisch Papers.

5

"Reverse Mission" among American Evangelicals

The last chapter showed that while the Trobisches were at the cutting edge of African marriage guidance in the 1960s, by the 1970s the African church had its own proponents who could carry the work forward. This chapter will show how the termination of Walter Trobisch's Lutheran World Federation contract in 1971 facilitated a turn to the United States.

The Trobisches had always kept one foot in the United States. Ingrid was American, and most of her family lived in the United States. However, while Walter was employed with the Lutheran World Federation (LWF) from 1968 to 1971, the focus of the Trobisches' work was on marriage guidance in Africa. With the termination of Walter's LWF contract, the Trobisches became freer from an occupational perspective and more needy financially. They began to spend a greater percentage of their time and to direct a greater percentage of their theological reflection to sexual guidance among evangelical college students in the United States. Their knowledge of African culture and their experience contextualizing the gospel in Africa enhanced their ability to conduct marriage guidance in the United States and increased their appeal.

In a process missiologists call "reverse mission," the Trobisches used the books, arguments, and spiritual practices they had developed for Africa in their growing ministry in the United States. They also brought African perspectives on femininity, fertility, childbirth, and breastfeeding to America to help evangelicals negotiate a more nuanced relationship with second wave feminism. The Trobisches' message resonated most with young, American evangelicals, who were struggling to make sense of the sexual revolution in light of their evangelical faith. The Trobisches gave these young evangelicals tools to navigate changing sexual norms and to express their faith through their sexual practices.

EVANGELICALS AND THE SEXUAL REVOLUTION

During the 1960s and 1970s, American sexual norms were changing rapidly. This was due to increasing numbers of women in the paid workforce, increasing numbers of women attending college, the availability of the birth control pill, and decreasing social stigma attached to premarital sex. According to historian Nancy Woloch, "During the 1960s, the number of women college students doubled." During the 1970s, "when almost 44 percent of the college-age population went to school, one-third of college-age women were enrolled."[1] The birth control pill came on the market in 1960. By 1962, 1.2 million women in American were taking the pill, and by 1965 that number had risen to 6.5 million.[2] Although some states prohibited distributing the pill to unmarried women, most women "who wanted birth control could usually find a way to get it."[3] The availability of the birth control pill facilitated a growing acceptance of premarital sex.[4]

The abandonment of *in loco parentis* rules at colleges and universities also facilitated the growing acceptance of premarital sex. Prior to 1965, most college officials in the United States could enforce curfews, dress codes, dorm visiting hours, and the like. In the early to mid 1960s, students began protesting these *in loco parentis* rules in earnest. "A 1964–65 survey of 850 colleges, including the 50 largest public universities, demonstrated that students felt the most important issues on campus were various *in loco parentis* rules."[5] In 1965, the administration at Michigan State University gave in to several of the students' demands; as the decade wore on, school after school abandoned *in loco parentis* rules.[6] Although *in loco parentis* rules had not stopped students from being sexually active, the rules had at least given a semblance of restriction on sexual activity. If girls had to be in their dorm by midnight, with boys strictly off the premises, a school could give the impression that its students were moral and self-controlled. Once

1. Woloch, *Women and the American Experience*, 506.
2. PBS, "Pill."
3. May, *America and the Pill*, 73.
4. Goode, *World Revolution and Family Patterns*, 37.
5. Anderson, *Movement and the Sixties*, 113.
6. Anderson, *Movement and the Sixties*, 112.

curfews were abolished, that vision was compromised, and young people had one less external structure deterring premarital sex.

Evangelical colleges held onto their *in loco parentis* rules longer than many state schools. However, evangelicals were not immune to the social ferment all around them. While their fundamentalist forebears had withdrawn from mainstream American culture after losing the modernist controversy of the 1920s, evangelicals in the 1960s and 1970s were far more willing to engage American culture. George Marsden has described how several leading fundamentalists during the 1950s became a "force for renewal and broadening of fundamentalism" and gradually reversed the separationist policies of fundamentalism.[7] According to Marsden, one strong sign of the success of these "neo-evangelicals" was the flourishing of evangelical colleges during the 1960s and 1970s.[8] Many fundamentalists during the 1930s and 1940s had viewed intellectual pursuits with suspicion.[9] The willingness on the part of numerous evangelicals during the 1960s and 1970s to send their children to college—albeit evangelical colleges—showed how much they had departed from their fundamentalist roots.

Evangelicals in the 1960s and 1970s encouraged college attendance, and the G.I. Bill made it economically feasible, but nothing really prepared young, college-bound evangelicals for the experience of relating modern youth culture to evangelical identity. Evangelical colleges like Wheaton and Westmont worked hard to assert their distinctive Christian identity. They required their faculty to be Christian and their students to sign pledges pertaining to proper behavior. Nevertheless, mainstream American youth culture made its way onto these campuses. Young evangelicals knew about Helen Gurley Brown, who in her 1962 bestseller, *Sex and the Single Girl*, unabashedly encouraged career women to enjoy sex with whomever they pleased, whenever they pleased. Evangelicals felt themselves being swept up in the spirit of the times, a spirit of "uninhibitedness, open discussion, self-fulfillment, and sexual free enterprise."[10] During the 1960s, the rate of premarital sex rose among non-evangelicals, and it is likely that this trend was mirrored in the evangelical community. At the very least, evangelical attitudes towards premarital sex loosened during the 1960s and 1970s.[11]

7. Marsden, *Reforming Fundamentalism*, 67.
8. Marsden, *Reforming Fundamentalism*, 11, 260.
9. Marsden, *Reforming Fundamentalism*, 10.
10. Woloch, *Women and the American Experience*, 507.
11. A survey distributed to Fuller Seminary graduates shows that 92 percent of students who attended Fuller between 1950 to 1952 found premarital sex "always" wrong. Only 77 percent of the 1965–67 class found premarital sex "always" wrong (Marsden,

Within Christian circles, the publication of John Robinson's book *Honest to God* further eroded the taboo against premarital sex. Robinson was a bishop in the Church of England. He argued that the Christian ethic best suited to the age was one in which "nothing [was] prescribed—except love."[12] This "love ethic" could be used in all ethical situations, but among college students it became especially associated with sexual morality. Robinson argued that it was inappropriate to simply assume that "'sex relations before marriage' . . . are wrong or sinful in themselves. They may be in 99 cases or even 100 cases out of 100, but they are not intrinsically so, for the only intrinsic evil is lack of love."[13]

According to Letha Scanzoni, an evangelical writer at the time, after Robinson's *Honest to God* came out, "Suddenly it seemed everyone was talking about 'relativism,' 'situational ethics,' 'freedom from legalism,' 'the love ethic,' 'the new morality,' 'the relationship ethic,' and so on."[14] Robinson caused such an uproar that a "conference on the sexual and marital aspects of the new morality" was held at Harvard Divinity School in the Spring of 1965 and was attended by some 500 Christian pastors and professors. Most of the attendees followed Robinson's lead and embraced "situational ethics" and the "love ethic." They argued that as long as "love for the neighbor is safeguarded, any type of behavior agreed upon by two adult persons is acceptable."[15] They suggested that young people should be educated on the use of contraceptives and should be encouraged to talk openly about the sexual component of their relationships. This open communication, it was thought, would help to dissipate misplaced guilt that was the result of an upbringing that prohibited premarital sex. After the Harvard conference, the evangelical editors of *Christianity Today* expressed their disgust with the general tenor of the conference. Most of the attendees at the conference had supported the perspective of the "new morality," but Carl Henry of *Christianity Today* embraced the opposing perspective: "The so-called new morality is as old as human evil and its advocacy at least as old as the classical pagan writers."[16]

Reforming Fundamentalism, 306).

12. Robinson, *Honest to God*, 116.
13. Robinson, *Honest to God*, 118.
14. Scanzoni, "New Morality," 241.
15. Henry, "Time for Moral Indignation," 29.
16. Henry, "Time for Moral Indignation," 30.

THE TROBISCHES' WORK WITH INTERVARSITY CHRISTIAN FELLOWSHIP

Alarmed by the growing acceptance of the new morality among college students, evangelical campus ministries began actively promoting premarital chastity. Campus Crusade for Christ (CCC) had always expected students to abide by a "fairly strict behavioral code," which entailed abstinence from "smoking, drinking, and premarital sex."[17] Prior to the 1960s, however, CCC did not spend much time addressing these issues in its ministry to college students. As talk of the new morality spread, however, one of CCC's popular speakers began giving talks on "Sex, Love, and Marriage."[18] He highlighted the importance of saving sex for marriage and argued that premarital sex would hurt one's future marriage. The campus ministry InterVarsity Christian Fellowship (IVCF) addressed premarital sex and the new morality in its student magazine, *HIS* in such articles as "How Does a Girl Decide" and "Dating: With or Without Petting."[19]

In 1964, IVCF published an English edition of Walter Trobisch's *J'ai Aimé Une Fille* in the March and April issues of *HIS*. In response to the article, Trobisch received a stream of letters from exuberant college students, requesting the book in paperback form. A reader from Wisconsin wrote, "Premarital relations are a major point of discussion and concern among students today. Rarely is a strong, articulate word such as this spoken for the standards God has set for us."[20] The editor of *HIS* wrote to Ingrid Trobisch, "I Loved a Girl has probably been the highlight of the year for HIS . . . Your husband seems to have the wave-length of American college students and we want more from his pen."[21]

Ingrid contacted Melvin Arnold, Director of the Religious Department at Harper & Row, whom she knew from her own book contract with Harper & Row. Arnold wrote to Lutterworth Press in London to obtain the American rights to publish *I Loved a Girl*. When *I Loved a Girl* came out in the United States in February of 1965, it was the first time that *I Loved a Girl* and its sequel *I Love a Young Man* appeared together in the same volume. The book sold well. In 1966 and 1967, Harper sold about two thousand copies per month.[22] In 1969, Melvin Arnold wrote to congratulate the

17. Turner, *Bill Bright and Campus Crusade for Christ*, 62.
18. Turner, *Bill Bright and Campus Crusade for Christ*, 124.
19. Gordon, "How Does a Girl Decide"; Small, "Dating."
20. W. and I. Trobisch to friends, September 1964, Missionary Personnel Files.
21. Quoted in I. Trobisch to Edward Sammis, 23 November 1964, Ingrid Trobisch Papers.
22. Hugh Van Dusen to I. Trobisch, 5 August 1966, Ingrid Trobisch Papers.

Trobisches. "I noticed a few days ago another big reprint going through," he wrote. "This brings us to 95,000 copies in print in this country alone. With 300,000 in print in Germany you must be either approaching the million mark or beyond it already."[23]

I Loved a Girl was, by far, the Trobisches' most successful book. However, three of Walter's other books were also well received by evangelical college students in the early 1970s: *Spiritual Dryness* (1970), *Love is a Feeling to be Learned* (1971), and *Love Yourself* (1975). All three books were published by InterVarsity Press (IVP), the printing arm of IVCF. According to Andy Le Peau, Associate Publisher at IVP, "[Walter's] books were among our better selling books for the era. In fact, *Love Yourself* was our number 1 book for the year in which it was released."[24]

Because of the success of Walter's books, in 1972 IVCF invited him to lecture at a number of North American colleges, most of which were small, Christian colleges.[25] During this tour, Walter got to see first-hand how "the booklets which we originally wrote for Africans were so widely read among American college students."[26] All his life, Walter had struggled with feelings of depression and doubt about his own self-worth. The termination of his contract with the LWF at the end of 1971 had not helped his propensity toward malaise. The trip to the United States in February of 1972 turned out to be a real ego-booster. At nearly every school he visited, "I was presented with a list of students who asked for an appointment even before my first lecture."[27] Although he would draw theological significance from this in his letters to supporters, he also drew a certain amount of personal pleasure from his apparent popularity among American college students. Moreover, he increasingly began to think of himself as a kind of celebrity.[28]

After his trip to the United States in February of 1972, Walter received invitations to speak at several small, Christian colleges. IVCF offered to fly the entire Trobisch family to the States during the summer of 1973, but the Trobisches decided the trip would be too hard on the children. "We see the danger that it might be even harder on our children when they find both parents present and at the same time completely absorbed by talks with

23. Melvin Arnold to I. Trobisch, 13 June 1969, Ingrid Trobisch Papers.
24. Le Peau, email, 9 August 2010.
25. Walter spoke to students at Trinity College, Redlands College, Westmont College, Seattle Pacific College, Carleton College, Hamline University, Bethel College, and the University of Minnesota (W. and I. Trobisch to friends, 9 March 1972, Ingrid Trobisch Papers).
26. W. and I. Trobisch to friends, 9 March 1972, Ingrid Trobisch Papers.
27. W. and I. Trobisch to friends, 9 March 1972, Ingrid Trobisch Papers.
28. D. Trobisch, interview, 4 September 2010.

other people," Walter wrote to the director of IVP.[29] The Trobisches' oldest daughter had by this point graduated from high school, but their remaining four children were still in school. The Trobisches decided to make the trip the following February, when the children had gone back to school.

In February of 1974, Walter spoke at Augsburg College and Barrington College. The Trobisches also led a family life seminar at Augustana Lutheran Church in Minneapolis. This church represented for the Trobisches the continuity of their life's work. Walter and Ingrid had met at Augustana College. Ingrid had been commissioned as a missionary with the Sudan Mission at Augustana Lutheran Church in Minneapolis. After the Trobisches founded FLM, the church processed contributions to FLM for them. On this visit in 1974, the couple was commissioned for their work in marriage counseling. Afterwards, the Trobisches flew to Jackson, Mississippi, to lead a seminar for student couples. Then Ingrid left and Walter led two retreats for couples in Georgia and Colorado.[30]

The Trobisches and the director of IVP, Jim Nyquist, felt that the best strategy for spreading the Trobisches' message about love, sex, and marriage would be for them to train IVCF staff to be "multipliers" of their message on college campuses. With this aim, the Trobisches led a seminar for several IVCF staff and spouses in Chicago in 1974. Walter discussed the content of the letters he had received since his last visit to the United States, since these letters revealed the major issues young people were facing on the college campuses where the IVCF staff worked. Walter also talked with the staff about the counseling techniques he used with students, since his one-on-one counseling sessions had proven helpful in empowering students to follow through with changes in their sexual behavior. The IVCF staff responded positively to the Trobisches' seminar and requested that it be duplicated for other staff members in years to come.

The decision of IVP to promote the Trobisches' books and counseling techniques among college students reinforced the Trobisches' new focus on the United States. In 1974, two American college students offered to come live with the Trobisches in order to help answer the letters from the United States.[31] In 1975, the Trobisches led seminars for IVCF staff in Chicago, Spokane, and St. Paul. Staff praised the Trobisches. "They held me spellbound," wrote Rebecca Herman. Jim Hibma said that after the seminar, he was "much more at ease in talking with students about their sexuality and

29. W. Trobisch to Jim Nyquist, 30 June 1972, Missionary Personnel Files.
30. W. and I. Trobisch to friends, October 1974, Ingrid Trobisch Papers.
31. Elizabeth Goldhor stayed for two years and Marie de Putron, for one (W. and I. Trobisch to friends, Easter 1975, Ingrid Trobisch Papers).

being able to guide them." Sid Lindmark praised Walter for being "concrete, specific and helpful."[32] Such positive feedback caused the IVCF to invite the Trobisches to give another seminar for IVCF staff in 1979 in Camp Spalding, Washington.[33]

During the 1970s the Trobisches received numerous invitations to speak in other venues, but they usually declined unless these invitations could be coordinated with IVCF trips. There were several reasons for this. First, independent trips to the United States continued to be inconceivable financially. Second, the Trobisches liked to reserve time in their schedule for writing literature, which they considered to be central to the work of FLM. Third, even though marriage guidance for the United States now formed an important component of their work, their interest in Africa always remained primary.

THE TROBISCHES' APPEAL AMONG AMERICAN EVANGELICALS

The remainder of this chapter will discuss reasons for the Trobisches' appeal among American evangelicals.

Frank Discussion of Sex

The Trobisches were some of the only evangelicals in the mid-twentieth century who were willing to talk about sex. A year after *I Loved a Girl* came out, Masters and Johnson electrified the American public with their publication of *Human Sexual Response*. And in 1972, Alex Comfort's *The Joy of Sex* was at the top of the New York Times bestseller list for eleven months.[34] In the evangelical world, however, it was still uncommon to speak or write about sex.[35] Letha Scanzoni was one of the few evangelical writers during the 1960s and 1970s who *was* willing to talk about sex.[36] She remembers the Trobisches and "the impact they were having on many young people in the 1960s and 1970s." She believes they were having such an impact "because of the Trobisches' open and frank discussion of topics many other Christians

32. Rebecca Herman, Jim Hibma, and Sid Lindmark, "Trobisch Seminar Evaluation," in Ron Nicholas to W. Trobisch, 13 October 1975, Missionary Personnel Files.

33. I. Trobisch to friends, March 1980, Ingrid Trobisch Papers.

34. Justice, *Bestseller Index*, 75.

35. Mace, *Christian Response to the Sexual Revolution*, 126–28.

36. See Scanzoni, *Sex and the Single Eye*; Scanzoni, *Sex Is a Parent Affair*; Scanzoni, *Why Wait?*

(evangelicals and Roman Catholics especially) hesitated to talk about at the time."[37] When Walter submitted his *I Loved a Girl* manuscript to Harper & Row, his editor likewise commented, "Curiously enough, there is very little frank, effective literature on this subject [sex]."[38]

The letters the Trobisches received suggest that young people found the Trobisches' discussion of sex helpful. As one young woman wrote to Ingrid, "I was ready to give up my virginity last night and then . . . I read your husband's article *I Loved a Girl* and want to thank him for his frank and helpful comments. It helped to reaffirm my own position and I now desire to 'save' myself for the young man whom I shall love someday."[39]

Defense of Premarital Chastity and Practical Advice for Remaining Chaste

Defending premarital chastity had been an important part of Walter's *J'ai Aimé Une Fille*, but the American context to which he and Ingrid turned their attention in the 1970s called for an even greater attention to this topic. Most young evangelicals in the 1960s and 1970s believed that premarital sex was a sin, but they were also drawn to the arguments of the new morality. The problem for them was knowing which sexual acts were allowable and which were not. Walter's correspondence with a young woman from Grace Bible College demonstrates the way in which young people accepted the new morality and attempted to blend it with traditional, Christian sexual ethics. The young woman, L.W., told Walter that although she had been "infatuated before . . . my present boyfriend and I feel we are in love."[40] She then elaborated on what she meant by love. "When I say 'in love' I mean that we experience the desires and emotions of love. I seek to meet my boyfriend's emotional needs; we share important things in our lives plus the trivial; we don't play threatening games to try and get the other one jealouse [sic], etc." L.W. described herself as a "strong Christian" even though she had what she knew to be a questionable sexual history, by Christian standards. Although she and her boyfriend had "never had intercourse," they had "done everything else." In her letter, L.W. seemed to justify the sexual component of her relationship by the fact that she and her boyfriend were "in love" and by the

---

37. Scanzoni, email, 2 February 2010.

38. Edward Sammis to Melvin Arnold, 9 November 1964, Ingrid Trobisch Papers.

39. Quoted in I. Trobisch to Michael Foxell, 4 February 1966, Ingrid Trobisch Papers.

40. L.W. to W. Trobisch, 20 September 1978, Walter Trobisch Collection, Box 1, Folder W.

fact that they were not "going all the way." Essentially, she was piecing together the old morality of chastity before marriage with the new love ethic.

In their books and lectures, the Trobisches cleared up any confusion about what was meant by "going all the way." They argued that heavy petting was not acceptable from a Christian perspective. "I know Christians who believe that they can outwit God in this way," wrote Walter. "After all, they have not gone 'all the way'!" He continued, "It does look like an ideal solution, but it isn't. It is barking up the wrong tree. It's a dead-end road."[41]

The Trobisches challenged students who argued that a Christian commitment to chastity was a legalistic doctrine violating the gospel of love. They argued that premarital chastity actually protected love by allowing it to develop in a gradual way. Having sex right away, they suggested, was like "picking the blossoms in April and therefore never harvesting the apples."[42] The Trobisches promised young people that remaining chaste prior to marriage would create a much more satisfying foundation for sex within marriage. They argued that, contrary to common opinion, the new morality degraded women rather than freeing them.[43]

Several of the letters the Trobisches received thanked them for their message, which sliced through the relativism of the age and called young people to premarital chastity. One young man said he had personally "suffered the consequences of the 'new morality'" and could therefore testify "to the critical need of your message for my contemporaries. Becoming a Christian in 1973, your books brought a new hope and balm to the cynicism this period brought about for me, and I know countless other American young people have similarly found comfort in your books."[44]

In lectures and books, the Trobisches shared stories from people with whom they had corresponded. Many of these people said they were dissatisfied with their decision to become sexually active. "I had a bad conscience when I said 'yes' to my boy friend," Karin told Walter. "I just pretended to be happy, but I really felt like sobbing and weeping."[45] In sharing stories like Karin's, the Trobisches hoped to encourage other young people to listen to their conscience and save sex for marriage.

Besides developing arguments for premarital chastity, the Trobisches also gave detailed, practical advice for *how* one could remain chaste. In his popular book *Love is a Feeling to be Learned,* Walter suggested that a basic

---

41. Trobisch, *Complete Works of Walter Trobisch*, 135.
42. Trobisch, *Complete Works of Walter Trobisch*, 127.
43. Trobisch, *Complete Works of Walter Trobisch*, 123.
44. W. H. to W. Trobisch, 4 September 1977, Ingrid Trobisch Papers.
45. Trobisch, *Complete Works of Walter Trobisch*, 136.

rule of thumb for remaining chaste would be to refrain from lying down and from undressing.[46] And in *I Loved a Girl,* Walter recommend channeling sexual energy into creative activities like writing, making music, or traveling.[47] This clear, practical advice was unique in the Christian world. Hans-Joachim Heil, a theology student who helped Walter with his books and correspondence, remembers that in Germany "there had been very few writers on themes like sex etc. [These writers] gave some theological reflections but didn't give practical help. Walter and Ingrid were the first to write and speak frankly . . . As counselors they had to be 'practical.' That's what nobody had done before, neither in Africa nor in Europe. And that's exactly what counselees need!"[48]

The Trobisches' Situational Approach to Counseling

During the 1970s, the Trobisches decided to tackle the topic of masturbation, which, like premarital sex, was receiving only scant attention from evangelicals of the period. The Trobisches had corresponded at length with a European woman who had asked for their help in overcoming her habit of masturbating. They obtained the young woman's permission to edit and publish the correspondence. In the book, the Trobisches encouraged the woman, Ilona, "to distinguish between necessary and unnecessary" masturbation:

> Our suggestion would be, for the time being, to set yourself a preliminary goal; in other words, to avoid m. [abbreviation for masturbation] when it is avoidable. . . . Only you can judge when m. is avoidable and when it is not. We are not your judges. It is very difficult to give any general rules about dealing with m. because sexual pressure is for some people stronger than others. . . . This is why one has to deal with each person differently and in a way you have to become your own 'therapist.'[49]

Throughout the book, the Trobisches helped Ilona (and others who read the correspondence) to analyze what masturbation was. They argued that it was a typical behavior, which corresponded to the "autoerotic" stage of development. Sex, they advised Ilona, was meant to be a means of communication between two people. Since masturbation only involved the self,

---

46. Trobisch, *Complete Works of Walter Trobisch,* 133.
47. Trobisch, *Complete Works of Walter Trobisch,* 41–43.
48. H. Heil, email, 22 November 2011.
49. Trobisch, *Complete Works of Walter Trobisch,* 282.

it was an inferior and immature form of sexuality.[50] The Trobisches also helped Ilona uncover why she felt the need to masturbate and gave her advice about how to gradually overcome her dependence on it.

The Trobisches' correspondence with Ilona illustrates another aspect of their appeal among American evangelicals. For most evangelicals, masturbation was simply wrong, case closed. For the Trobisches, it was "very difficult to give any general rules" about masturbation. They believed masturbation was wrong, but they recognized that individual counselees had different needs and different abilities and were at different stages in their spiritual journeys.[51] They took these things into consideration when they counseled people.

One of the IVCF staff members who attended a Trobisch seminar in 1975 took note of their situational approach to counseling. She remembered Walter constantly telling them, "Now, don't be legalistic about this—you don't always have to do it this way."[52] Another helpful example of this situational approach to counseling can be found in Trobisch's correspondence with an InterVarsity worker in Cameroon. She had written to him in order to ask, "Please could you tell me whether what is sometimes called 'petting to climax' is a sin when the two people concerned are not married."[53] Trobisch responded by asking her a series of questions about herself and her boyfriend. After doing so he said, "I apologize to you for asking all these questions. But I do not ask them out of curiosity. It is easy to set up a law and then say: that's it. But in order to really help you I have to know your situation and your story, and then I think I can find the answer which Christ has prepared for you and for your personal way."[54]

As was previously mentioned, a situational approach to sexual ethics became popular among Christians after the publication of Bishop Robinson's book, *Honest to God*. Although Trobisch never allowed the situational approach to justify premarital sex, as some Christians were doing, his use of the situational approach to sexual ethics earned him a hearing with those who found the situational approach appealing. In effect, Trobisch's approach bore enough similarity to the relativistic sexual climate of mainstream America to make it seem fresh and cutting edge. However,

---

50. Trobisch, *Complete Works of Walter Trobisch*, 270–74.

51. Trobisch, *Complete Works of Walter Trobisch*, 257.

52. Rebecca Herman, "Trobisch Seminar Evaluation," in Ron Nicholas to W. Trobisch, 13 October 1975, Missionary Personnel Files.

53. M. B. to W. Trobisch, 20 October 1968, Walter Trobisch Collection, Box 14, Folder B.

54. W. Trobisch to M. B., 28 January 1969, Walter Trobisch Collection, Box 14, Folder B.

by refusing to surrender Christian sexual ideals like premarital chastity, he conveyed a sense of the uniqueness of evangelical Christian identity. This approach fit well with the developing consciousness of evangelicals who, during the 1970s, wanted to both engage American culture as well as distinguish themselves from it.

Trobisch knew his situational approach to sexual ethics would be criticized by conservative evangelicals, but this did not stop him from using it. He wrote in the preface to his book on masturbation, "We know in advance that our comments will be too conservative for the 'liberals' and too liberal for the 'conservatives.'"[55] As long as he believed what he was doing was right, Trobisch had never been afraid of offending people. He especially did not mind offending church elders if it gained him a hearing among Christian youth. For example after a trip to Africa, he had remarked, "Generally, we had the choice of either offending the older generation, including pastors and church leaders, by being too 'frank', or of being accused by the younger generation of hiding information from them. Therefore we chose the first alternative, foreseeing the danger of the church losing contact with the younger generation by the inflexibility of some of their leaders."[56] Trobisch believed that an inflexible position on masturbation would simply alienate the young people he sought to address. He believed that only full disclosure would help them process and move beyond masturbation. He was willing to take criticism from older evangelicals for being too flexible or too frank in his advice if it meant preserving a relationship with the younger generation.

Trobisch had initially fallen into a situational approach to sexual ethics in Africa when he began to reflect on the inadequacy of the church's response to the practice of polygamy. He argued that polygamy "cannot be dealt with in a general way. We rather have to decide individually and deal with every single case separately."[57] This was essentially the same approach he took with the issue of masturbation. He believed it, like polygamy, was not ideal, but he also believed that issuing a blanket condemnation of the practice was not the most effective way to bring people into a deeper relationship with Christ, which was his ultimate aim as a missionary. "To help the individual in the name of the God of peace we need both the rules *and* the exceptions," he said.[58]

---

55. Trobisch, *Complete Works of Walter Trobisch*, 259.

56. W. Trobisch, "Report on trip to Cameroun October–November 1969," Missionary Personnel Files.

57. W. Trobisch to Paul Hansen, 14 December 1963, Ingrid Trobisch Papers.

58. Trobisch, "Congregational Responsibility for the Christian Individual," 106.

An Invitation to Confess

So many of the people who met with Trobisch while he was on their college campus or who wrote to him after reading his books believed that premarital sex was wrong, but despite this belief they continued to be sexually active. Thus they were plagued by guilt and low self-esteem. One young woman told Trobisch that since her boyfriend and she "couldn't marry right away [they] began some pretty heavy petting to try to satisfy our desires. It only brought further frustrations and some terrible terrible guilt feelings on both of our parts."[59] Still, they lacked the resolve to change their behavior. Trobisch invited young people like these to confess their sexual sin and seek to live a new life.

After his trip to the United States in 1972, Trobisch remarked, "The greatest need on all the campuses I visited was the cry for forgiveness."[60] In the years to come, the letters Trobisch received from numerous students expressed the same cry. And they attested to the relief that confession and forgiveness granted. One young woman told Trobisch that she felt "a great sense of freedom since confessing my sins to you."[61] She also said her confession had helped her know what to say to a friend of hers who had "an overwhelming desire to confess." Another woman confessed to Trobisch her habit of masturbating. She then wrote him a letter expressing how good confession made her feel: "I felt a great relief and I praise the Lord for the time I spent with you that weekend."[62]

As Lutherans accustomed to the practice of confession in the weekly church worship service, applying confession to a parachurch situation came naturally to the Trobisches. Confession and forgiveness had also long been personally important to Walter, who had struggled with guilt and self-reproach and had found confession liberating.[63] Confession had also proven relevant in the Trobisches' work with Africans. For one thing, confession was an important part of African spiritual practice, both in African traditional religions and in the East African Revival of the early twentieth century.[64] Walter found that many of the Africans who wrote to him did so in order "to obtain forgiveness for something they regretted doing."[65]

    59. K. M. to W. Trobisch, 29 January 1979, Walter Trobisch Collection, Box 1.
    60. W. and I. Trobisch to friends, 9 March 1972, Ingrid Trobisch Papers.
    61. M. W. to W. Trobisch, 22 March 1979, Walter Trobisch Collection, Box 1.
    62. K. M. to W. Trobisch, 29 January 1979, Walter Trobisch Collection, Box 1.
    63. He spoke about confession in his series of talks for the annual conference of the Sudan Mission in 1954 and wrote often about confession during the 1960s and 1970s.
    64. Karanja, "Confession and Cultural Dynamism."
    65. Banyolak, "Africa Needs Marriage Counsellors," 67–68.

Formal confession was not standard liturgical practice in most American evangelical churches of the time, but the Trobisches found that the practice was helpful in responding to the results of the sexual revolution. The evangelical students Walter counseled showed him time and again that they craved moral standards.[66] They thanked Trobisch for debunking the new morality and defending the ideal of premarital chastity, and they welcomed his offer to confess sexual sin.

DOING "REVERSE MISSION"

Conveying the Message of the Cross through *J'ai Aimé Une Fille*

Walter Trobisch's use of confession in the counseling process and his dedication to a situational approach to counseling both demonstrate his use of "reverse mission," as he was taking approaches he had learned in Africa and was applying them to his work in the West. Trobisch's negotiation of the contract for the American edition of *J'ai Aimé Une Fille* also demonstrates how he brought insight from Africa to the United States. First, Trobisch's editor at Harper & Row suggested Americanizing the characters. Trobisch would have no such thing: "I would never agree to making the American edition an 'Americanized edition.' I'm sure that one of the reasons for its appeal to American young people is that it's addressed to Africans and not to Americans directly which would make young people rebel only."[67] Trobisch believed the story would only be successful in accomplishing its aim (which, in the United States, was far more about promoting premarital chastity than exposing bride-price abuses) if it kept the African storyline. By articulating a message about premarital chastity in relation to African customs like the bride-price and arranged marriage, Trobisch believed this classic Christian ethic would be more well-received.

Second, Trobisch had found in Africa that the text's genre also appealed to readers and helped to convey his goals. Using story rather than essay allowed Trobisch to communicate the complexities of making moral decisions. This, too, was a way the American edition of *J'ai Aimé Une Fille* brought insights from Africa to America. *J'ai Aimé Une Fille* did not present an abstract list of rules that should be followed in order to pursue

---

66. Trobisch wrote to his editor the following: "Young people today, (although they don't admit it) are longing for rules—maybe for only one reason—to have something which they can overstep. It is merciless in a world where all rules have broken down to refuse to give rules and simply say: Rely upon your conscience" (W. Trobisch to Edward Sammis, 7 April 1964, Ingrid Trobisch Papers).

67. W. Trobisch to Edward Sammis, 7 April 1964, Ingrid Trobisch Papers.

the Christian life. Rather, it presented the moral ambiguities of life in the modern world and the ways in which young people in a different part of the world were seeking to navigate a fulfilling and morally upright life. The story was also presented as a series of letters, which gave it a sense of rawness and urgency. The story did not seem over-processed, cleaned up, and smoothed out around the edges. This attribute had drawn African young people to *J'ai Aimé Une Fille*, and it likely had the same effect on American young people.

J'ai Aimé Une Fille ended in tragedy. François and Cecile fail to convince Cecile's father to lower the bride-price he demands for his daughter. Since paying the bride-price will put François into massive debt, the lovers feel they have no choice but to elope. Trobisch believed the tragic ending of *J'ai Aimé Une Fille* was part of the reason people were drawn to the book. It communicated the fact that things do not always work out in the end. Trobisch's editor at Harper & Row actually recommended changing the tragic ending of the story. Rather than having the lovers elope, the editor favored a restoration of the relationship with Cecile's father. Trobisch refused to change the text. He argued that the tragic ending made the story more attractive to readers. "Excuse me for saying this," he wrote to the American editor, "but your reaction is typically American, because the American lacks a sense of tragedy. Everything has to work." He went on, "I am sure that the negative ending . . . counts at least partly for its success. In the moment you give a 'happy ending' it becomes a cheap Christian tract where two and two make four."[68] The discussion over the happy ending continued over a span of months, and Trobisch stood his ground.

At stake, for Trobisch, was the truth of the gospel: "A happy-end," he said, suggested theologically that "all problems can be solved":

> Consequently if you have unsolved problems, you do not believe, God is not with you . . . In contrast to this I want to show in my book how to live close to God with conflicts, how to exist as a Christian before an impossibility . . . I believe that this message, that God is with him in his dilemma . . . is the essential Christian message—the message of the Cross, while the happy-end theology is not only not helpful, but even disastrous and the denial of the Living God.[69]

In the end, *I Loved a Girl* went to press with the tragic ending. Trobisch was able to bring "the message of the Cross" from Africa to North America. The editors did, however, get Trobisch to compromise a little. They had Trobisch write a pastoral note "To the Reader," in which he explained the tragic

---

68. W. Trobisch to Edward Sammis, 7 April 1964, Ingrid Trobisch Papers.
69. W. Trobisch to Melvin Arnold, 23 November 1964, Ingrid Trobisch Papers.

ending and gave some theological advice for living before God in the midst of discouraging circumstances.

Ingrid Trobisch's Promotion of Natural Family Planning, Natural Childbirth, and Breastfeeding

While Walter was working on bringing "the message of the Cross" from Africa to North America, Ingrid Trobisch was working on bringing African ideas about femininity, childbirth, and breastfeeding. She had long been working to bring the latest information on the sympto-thermal method of Natural Family Planning (NFP) to African couples, so as to enable them to resume sexual relations earlier than the customary two years after the birth of a child. In 1973, she and Walter attended an International Symposium on Natural Family Planning.[70] At this meeting, the International Federation for Family Life Promotion (IFFLP) was established. Ingrid spoke at an IFFLP conference in Florence, Italy the following year.

As Ingrid interacted with people at international conferences and at marriage seminars she and Walter led for couples in Europe, she began to realize that many Westerners were just as interested in natural means of birth control as Africans.[71] Despite the availability of condoms, IUDs, and the birth control pill, Ingrid found that many people "were ill at ease with the methods offered to them in dealing with their fertility."[72] The prevalence of abortion proved to her that people were not satisfied with the birth control methods available. "If the proposed methods of conception control were as safe and as satisfying in their application as is often claimed," wrote Ingrid, "the problem of unwanted pregnancies should actually no longer exist."[73] With these things in mind, Ingrid began to rework her "Understanding Your Wife" series for a Western audience.[74] In the process of con-

---

70. Trobisch, *Joy of Being a Woman*, 60–61.

71. They gave premarital education to several European couples and led family life seminars for married couples in Austria and Germany ("Biographical Profile," Human Life Foundation," Ingrid Trobisch Papers).

72. Trobisch, *Joy of Being a Woman*, 43. Hesitancy to use the pill or the IUD was partly due to the side-effects and health risks associated with these methods. Pill use grew steadily during the 1960s, but in the late 1960s concerns about its safety came to the fore (especially after the publication of Barbara Seaman's book *The Doctors' Case against the Pill* in 1969). After 1973, the number of pill-users began to decline. Also during this time, IUDs were causing illness in hundreds of women and even led to the death of eighteen women (Tone, *Devices and Desires*, 203, 47, 49, 71).

73. Trobisch, *Joy of Being a Woman*, 43.

74. Originally, the Trobisches envisioned this series being read by African husbands

ducting research for her book, she visited the headquarters of SERENA, a Canadian organization dedicated to teaching couples NFP.[75] The success of this organization during the 1960s and 1970s further convinced Ingrid that there was a growing desire in the West for natural means of birth control.

Ingrid first published her "Understanding Your Wife" series in German through Editions Trobisch, the publishing arm of Family Life Mission. In 1974, she published the five booklets as a single text, *Mit Freuden Frau sein*. After it was well received in Germany, Ingrid began negotiations with Harper & Row for its publication in the United States. Harper & Row released the book in 1975 under the title *The Joy of Being a Woman . . . And What a Man Can Do*. Again, the book was well received. It was soon published in French, Spanish, Danish, Slovenian, Dutch, Polish, and Amharic.[76]

When Ingrid published *The Joy of Being a Woman,* Walter called it the first sex manual to be written by a woman.[77] This was not strictly true, but it *was* the first sex manual written by an evangelical woman. In the 1970s, non-evangelical women were turning to a book called *Our Bodies, Ourselves* for information about female sexuality, birth control, pregnancy, childbirth, breastfeeding, and other women's health issues. Published by a group of Boston women who were frustrated by the lack of information on these topics, the book sold a remarkable 250,000 copies between 1970 and 1973.[78] When Ingrid's *The Joy of Being a Woman* came out in 1975, it was the first book to discuss female sexuality, birth control, pregnancy, childbirth, breastfeeding, and menopause from a Christian woman's perspective. A sex manual by the popular evangelical couple Tim and Beverly LaHaye also came out in 1976, but it was more narrowly focused on birth control and sex and did not cover the whole lifecycle of a woman.[79]

After the publication of *The Joy of Being a Woman*, Ingrid received numerous letters from Western readers requesting more information about NFP. This confirmed her suspicions about the widespread discontent with condoms, the pill, and other artificial forms of birth control. It also stimulated her to take her role as an NFP promoter even more seriously. Because of her relationship with Joseph Roetzer and others pioneers in NFP research, such as Drs. John and Evelyn Billings, Ingrid was aware of the most

---

in order to better understand their wives (see p. 79).
75. W. and I. Trobisch to friends, October 1974, Ingrid Trobisch Papers.
76. W. and I. Trobisch to M. S. Mikhail, 17 January 1974, Ingrid Trobisch Papers.
77. Trobisch, *Joy of Being a Woman*, x.
78. The Boston Women's Health Book Collective, *Our Bodies, Ourselves*, 11.
79. LaHaye and LaHaye, *Act of Marriage*.

up-to-date research on NFP.[80] She worked this research into a sequel to *The Joy of Being a Woman*, which she co-authored with Dr. Roetzer's daughter, Elizabeth.[81] This book was essentially a question-and-answer guide to using NFP. It answered criticism from people who said the method was unreliable, shared testimonies from people who were pleased with the method, and included sample charts from women who had used NFP successfully and unsuccessfully.

Ingrid was a pioneer in promoting NFP among Western Protestants. John and Sheila Kippley, Catholic advocates of NFP, called *The Joy of Being a Woman* the first Protestant book to support NFP.[82] After its publication, "both Walter and Ingrid soon became welcomed speakers within the growing NFP community."[83] In 1977, another well-known Protestant couple, Larry and Nordis Christianson, advocated NFP in their primer on Christian marriage. They echoed Ingrid's argument that NFP enhanced personal and marital satisfaction by helping a woman to "live in harmony with her cycle."[84]

The description in the Christianson's book about how they came to be aware of NFP and why they liked it sheds light on why other American evangelicals in this period were interested in NFP. The Christiansons wrote, "When we were married in 1951, we didn't consider very deeply or seriously how to limit our family. We probably started out like most Protestant couples of that era. I went to the doctor for a premarital exam and was fitted with a contraceptive device . . . Later we came to feel that our experience with commonly used contraceptives was not entirely satisfactory."[85] Nordis got in touch with Dr. Konald A. Prem, who taught them about NFP. And when they began using NFP, their experience of sex improved. Nordis wrote, "We love and delight in each other more. Sexuality has become a more enjoyable, natural part of my life."[86] Most evangelicals in the 1960s and 1970s were thankful for the availability of the birth control pill and had

---

80. Drs. John and Evelyn Billings developed and promoted a method of NFP which relied on analysis of cervical mucus to determine fertile and non-fertile days (Billings, "Quest").

81. *Mit Freuden Frau sein 2* was translated into English as *An Experience of Love: Understanding Natural Family Planning*.

82. The Kippleys founded the Couple to Couple League to teach couples NFP (The Couple to Couple League, "About CCL").

83. Natural Family Planning International, "Not Just for Catholics," para. 17.

84. Christenson and Christenson, *Christian Couple*, 85.

85. Christenson and Christenson, *Christian Couple*, 71–72.

86. Christenson and Christenson, *Christian Couple*, 74.

no qualms about its use among married couples.⁸⁷ But for those who felt that the pill "was not entirely satisfactory," NFP was an attractive alternative, especially when it was promoted with convincing, scriptural arguments by well-known evangelicals like the Trobisches and the Christiansons.

Evangelical interest in NFP in the 1960s and 1970s can be seen as part of a wider North American movement against the medicalization of pregnancy and birth. Between 1750 and 1950, physicians had increasingly taken the place of midwives in the birth process and women were told to have their babies in hospitals.⁸⁸ Between the 1930s and 1960s, it was normal for women to be fully anesthetized with "twilight sleep" during childbirth. This treatment erased any memory of the experience of childbirth. During the 1950s, however, some women began to desire a more active childbirth experience.⁸⁹ They eagerly read books like Marjorie Karmel's *Thank You, Dr. Lamaze*, which described her birth experience with the French Dr. Fernand Lamaze. Dr. Lamaze had developed a method of childbirth that consisted of "childbirth education classes, relaxation, breathing techniques and continuous emotional support from the father."⁹⁰ In the 1960s, more books were published and organizations founded to support the natural childbirth movement.⁹¹ By the 1970s, expectant couples who were interested in natural childbirth had numerous books to choose from and support groups to join.

As the natural childbirth movement got underway, a movement to reinstate breastfeeding also took off. In the 1950s, most women bottle-fed their baby with formula, rather than breastfeeding. In 1956, only 21 percent of American mothers "left the hospital nursing their infants," and 62 percent of mothers had decided only to bottle-feed.⁹² Frustrated by this trend, a group of women in Chicago formed an organization to encourage women to breastfeed. They called their organization La Leche League and in 1958 published the first edition of *The Womanly Art of Breastfeeding*. By 1964, La Leche League groups were meeting in the United States, Canada, Mexico, and New Zealand.

The connections among the movements for natural childbirth, breastfeeding, and NFP are clear. People had grown frustrated by the medicalization and commoditization of fertility, pregnancy, and birth. They wanted

---

87. In 1968, twenty-five evangelical scholars signed "A Protestant Affirmation on the Control of Human Reproduction."

88. Leavitt, *Brought to Bed*, 3.

89. Plant, *Mom*, 136.

90. Harmon, "Happy 60th Birthday Lamaze International!," para. 3.

91. Kitzinger, *Experience of Childbirth*; Bradley, *Husband-Coached Childbirth*.

92. Cone, *200 Years of Feeding Infants in America*, 86.

to affirm women in their natural capabilities. As Ingrid asked in *The Joy of Being a Woman,* "Why should a healthy and normal woman be forced to become a patient when she wants to deal with her fertility?"[93]

In family life seminars with Walter, Ingrid gave the most up-to-date information about NFP. In *The Joy of Being a Woman,* she brought the work of SERNEA, Lamaze International, and La Leche League to the attention of the evangelical community. She pointed evangelical women to the resources available to them in these organizations. Since the organizations were not explicitly Christian, Ingrid's book was helpful for many evangelical women in the way it advocated NFP, natural childbirth, and breastfeeding from a Christian perspective.[94] Women could find information about women's health issues in *Our Bodies, Ourselves.* But many evangelical women would have been uncomfortable using this book since it was clearly the product of the feminist movement and had no problem with masturbation, homosexuality, and abortion.[95] For evangelical women, *The Joy of Being a Woman* offered a more conservative, but still informative, introduction to sexuality and women's health issues.

In her work promoting natural childbirth and breastfeeding, Ingrid was doing reverse mission. African women had taught her the profound capacity of women to give birth without the aid of anesthesia. These same African women had nursed their babies for two years, and Ingrid passed on their wisdom to Western evangelicals. She also passed on information about women's health and fertility from organizations like SERNEA, Lamaze International, and La Leche League.

Feminism from Africa

Ingrid and Walter Trobisch also brought a form of feminism from Africa to North America. When *The Joy of Being a Woman* came out in 1975, American evangelicals were in the midst of a heated debate about the role of women in church, family, and society.[96] Conservative evangelicals

---

93. Trobisch, *Joy of Being a Woman,* 53.

94. For the rest of her life, Ingrid promoted NFP and natural childbirth. In 1976, she spoke at the International Childbirth Education Association and at an International Symposium on NFP. In 1977, she spoke at the International Federation for Family Life Promotion (IFFLP) and at the International Society for Study of Prenatal Psychology. From 1980 to 1986, she sat on the Board of the IFFLP ("Activities, Summer 1976," Walter Trobisch Collection, Box 20; Trobisch, *My Journey Homeward,* 24, 163).

95. The Boston Women's Health Book Collective, *Our Bodies, Ourselves,* 47, 81–97, 216–38.

96. The "woman question" was one of the most important factors in forming

perceived a major incongruity between feminist and biblical views of gender and were uncomfortable with the tendency among feminists to minimize the differences between men and women. Progressive evangelicals, calling themselves Christian feminists, believed the Bible supported gender equality in church, marriage, and society. The Trobisches held a position on women that was strongly informed by their work in Africa and was, therefore, not easily pigeonholed into American categories. They were certainly aware of women's oppression and fought against it in Africa. In this sense, they were feminists. But, as the previous section made clear, their time in Africa also made them less willing than second wave feminists to impede the natural processes of pregnancy, childbirth, and breastfeeding.

Fighting against male dominance in African marital practices was a central part of the Trobisches' mission in Africa. As was explained in chapter 4, the Trobisches tended to use garden imagery to describe African marital practices. To put it crudely, the husband planted his seed in the wife's garden. The Trobisches believed this "garden concept of marriage" contributed strongly to the oppression of women because it dehumanized them, justified polygamy (a man can have many "gardens"), and legitimated divorce for infertility.[97] The Trobisches were therefore convinced that their "main mission in Africa was to replace the image of a woman as a 'thing' or a 'fruitful garden' with the contrasting image that expresses her humanity and individuality and the fact that she is made in the image of God, just as man is."[98] One way Walter advocated the full humanity of women was by asserting a woman's right to sexual fulfillment.[99] He even researched how "Kegel" exercises might help clitoridectomized women to achieve orgasm.

The Trobisches carried their awareness of female oppression with them when they spoke and wrote to Westerners. Given the persistence of male dominance in African marriages and the practice of clitoridectomy, the Trobisches generally considered Western women to be better off than African women. However, the Trobisches also believed that some discrimination against women persisted in Western society. In a letter to a colleague, Walter wrote, "As a matter of principle, I would be very glad from now on in your correspondence if you would always refer to both of us. In European

---

evangelical identity in the 1970s (Stasson, "Politicization of Family Life," 102).

97. Trobisch, *Complete Works of Walter Trobisch*, 387.

98. Trobisch, *My Journey Homeward*, 86.

99. He wrote in the introduction to Banyolak's *My Wife Has Lost Interest in Sex*, "In many African societies, especially also among Moslems, sexual pleasure is considered as a male privilege only. To declare that a woman too is entitled to sexual enjoyment and fulfillment is, as far as Africa is concerned, revolutionary in itself."

society we still have a discrimination of women and this is unfortunately also very evident in the Christian Church."[100]

This awareness of discrimination against women and desire to root it out put the Trobisches in the company of American Christian feminists like Letha Scanzoni, Nancy Hardesty, and Paul Jewett.[101] However, the Trobisches departed from the American Christian feminists in their determination to assert femininity and masculinity against the perceived threat of androgyny. As Ingrid wrote in *The Joy of Being a Woman*, "There are two kinds of women's movements today: those which try to eradicate the differences between the sexes and urge women to be like men, and those which fully appreciate the uniqueness of womanhood. I want to dedicate this book to the latter group. I want to help the liberated woman to retain her femininity."[102] The Trobisches believed God had created men and women with unique traits and roles. For example, when they encountered young women who were wearing pants, they often encouraged these women to wear a skirt instead. They saw skirt-wearing as a sign that a woman was secure in her God-given identity as a woman.[103] They were also content with the allocation of certain societal roles to certain sexes. Thus, when one of their sons asked Walter, "Do you have to be a pastor if you want to be a missionary?" Walter replied, "No, you certainly don't . . . You can be a doctor, a builder, a mechanic, or even an airplane pilot. And a girl can be a nurse or a teacher."[104]

Celebrating femininity and masculinity and urging certain gender roles put the Trobisches in the company of conservative, American evangelicals like James Dobson, Bill Gothard, and Marabel Morgan. These evangelicals encouraged husbands to lead and wives to submit. They opposed the Equal Rights Amendment because they believed it eradicated too many of the God-given differences between men and women.[105] And in 1977, they held a 15,000-strong "Pro-Family Rally" to express their opposition to the ERA, abortion, and gay rights.[106]

However, the Trobisches were nowhere near as opposed to the feminist movement as were these conservative evangelicals. Conservative

---

100. W. Trobisch to Pastor Axel-Ivar Berglund, 20 December 1968, Missionary Personnel Files.

101. Scanzoni and Hardesty, *All We're Meant to Be*; Jewett, *Man as Male and Female*.

102. Trobisch, *Joy of Being a Woman*, xi.

103. Trobisch, *Complete Works of Walter Trobisch*, 288.

104. Trobisch and Trobisch, *Adventures of Pumpelhoober*, 19.

105. Mathews and De Hart, *Sex, Gender, and the Politics of ERA*, 162.

106. Martin, *With God on Our Side*, 163, 65.

evangelicals have a history of uniting around a common enemy, and in the 1970s that enemy was feminism.[107] Conservative evangelicals blamed the feminist movement "for abortion, the rising divorce rate, the proliferation of sexually transmitted diseases . . . and a general moral decline in the country."[108] They believed that the way to restore healthy family life in America was for men and women to uphold the male-breadwinner, female-housewife gender roles.[109]

The Trobisches did not assert women's submission in marriage as the best way of restoring healthy family life. Rather, they held that communication and forgiveness would be far more effective in improving marital relationships. Walter had a story he liked to tell about the importance of communication and forgiveness. On one of their trips to Africa to lead a marriage seminar, Walter was so busy meeting with counselees and telling them how to improve their marriages that he neglected his own. Ingrid confronted him, and they proceeded to spend some quality time together.[110] This story did not depict the submissive wife described in conservative evangelical literature of the day. On the contrary, the Trobisches' stories expressed the importance of a wife being assertive.

Thus the Trobisches departed from conservative American evangelicals by teaching that it was possible and desirable for a Christian woman to be both feminine and independent. While Marabel Morgan taught women to subsume their own identity into that of their husband and Bill Gothard taught that the "chain of command" in marriage ran from God to man to woman, the Trobisches taught that a woman could have her own identity, could have career goals outside the sphere of being a good wife and mother, and could have ambition to reach these goals. This message did not attract crowds comparable to those generated by Marabel Morgan and Bill Gothard.[111] However, because their message was a more nuanced message than the strict hierarchy proclaimed by conservatives, the Trobisches could reach a more diverse audience. By advocating a woman's joy in marriage and motherhood, the Trobisches won themselves favor among conservative evangelicals who clung to traditional roles. Their affirmation of femininity assured conservative readers that they appreciated the God-given uniqueness

107. Lindsay, *Faith in the Halls of Power*, 52.
108. Balmer, *Blessed Assurance*, 88.
109. Davis, *More Perfect Unions*, 177–78.
110. Trobisch, *Complete Works of Walter Trobisch*, 489–94.
111. "It was not unusual in the 1970s for Gothard to pack-out auditoriums with capacities of 10,000 to 20,000 people." And Marabel Morgan's *The Total Woman* was "the best-selling nonfiction book of 1974," selling more than 3 million copies between 1974 and 1977 (Beardsley, "Bill Gothard"; Davis, *More Perfect Unions*, 204).

of the sexes. However, by advocating marital partnership and a woman's right to have interests outside the home, the Trobisches also made their message attractive to progressive evangelicals and mainline Protestants.

In the 1970s, both the Trobisches and IVCF strove to maintain the tension between femininity and female independence and thus avoided being characterized as either conservative or liberal. In their history of IVCF, Keith and Gladys Hunt have argued that the British roots of IVCF protected it from being characterized as either conservative or liberal. "IV student work was seen as an import, and as such it did not have ties to anything that was suspect to either the conservatives or the liberals."[112] Similarly, the Trobisches' international and missionary identity protected them somewhat from being characterized as conservative or liberal. And it was their missionary experience in Africa that had initially clued them in to male dominance and female oppression. Through their marriage counseling work in Africa and through Walter's study of clitoridectomy and female sexual response, the Trobisches worked for women's liberation. As they turned their attention to North America, they continued to be sensitive to women's oppression and to fight against it, but their view of that oppression differed slightly from that of other Christian feminists. Most Christian feminists of the 1970s were primarily concerned with advocating gender equality in church, family, and society. Celebrating the differences between men and women was seen as a more conservative pursuit. The Trobisches, however, believed that the loss of female distinctiveness and the failure to celebrate natural bodily processes associated with being female—menstruation, pregnancy, childbirth, nursing—were all ways that women in the West were being oppressed. Once again, this appreciation of natural female bodily processes was something that Ingrid had first learned from the women in Tchollire, Cameroon.

---

112. Hunt and Hunt, *For Christ and the University*, 93.

Conclusion

The Trobisches as Shapers of Global, Christian Sexual Ethics in the Mid-Twentieth Century

During the 1950s, 1960s, and 1970s, the Trobisches developed a message about sex, love, and marriage that blended feminist, Christian, African, and Western ideals. Although the Trobisches held paternalistic attitudes common among Western missionaries of their generation, their vision of sexuality helped Christians around the world to navigate changing sexual and marital norms of the mid-twentieth century. The Trobisches gained worldwide acclaim with Walter's book *J'ai Aimé Une Fille.* They influenced global sexual ideals and behavior through this book and others, as well as through their extensive correspondence ministry. In both Africa and in the United States they shaped theological reflection about sexual ethics and also influenced larger cultural conversations about sexuality in the modern world.

COMPARING SEXUAL ETHICS IN MID-TWENTIETH-CENTURY AFRICA AND AMERICA

The Trobisches' story demonstrates that young people in urban Africa had a lot in common with college-aged evangelicals in America during the mid-twentieth century. Education brought about changes in sexual ethics in both places during this time. In the United States, "the number of women college students doubled" in the 1960s.[1] Even fundamentalists, who had traditionally been hesitant to send their children to college, began to do so. The

---

1. Woloch, *Women and the American Experience,* 506.

presence of newly independent, unmarried evangelicals mingling together in a coeducational environment created a context not unlike that of mid-twentieth-century Africa, where young people from rural backgrounds moved to the city to attend school. In both contexts, the strict sexual norms young people had grown up with did not seem to apply to their new context.

In Africa, nationalist movements, the independence of young people from extended kin networks, and the need to figure out how to navigate life on their own bred a desire for independence in interpersonal relationships as well. Young people began expressing the desire to choose their own spouse. The Trobisches strongly approved of the right to choose one's own spouse and encouraged young people to do so in their books and personal counseling.

The desire for personal choice was also central to the changes in sexual practices in the United States. There the desire to choose was expressed most strongly in women's use of the birth control pill, which allowed them to regulate when and how many children to have. Even though the Trobisches preferred the natural family planning method of birth control over the birth control pill, they still approved of the right of couples to choose when and how many children to have. And they affirmed this right as they counseled both Africans and Americans on the issue of family planning.

Another trend uniting Africans and Americans during this period was the changing definition of womanhood. No longer was womanhood to be solely or primarily defined by the ability to have and raise children. Even as this theoretical definition of womanhood continued to be supported in both Africa and evangelical communities in the United States, the actual lives of individual women in both locations challenged the definition. For example, educated women in Africa often married later and had fewer children.[2] In the United States, the birth control pill allowed women to effectively separate sex from procreation, so they too began to have fewer children. The feminist movement further encouraged women to find their identity outside of home, children, and husband, and to enter the realm of paid employment. For their part, the Trobisches supported this changing definition of womanhood. They believed valuing women primarily for their ability to bring forth children objectified women. They used their books and letters to advocate for women's humanity as a more fundamental characteristic than their fecundity.

The Trobisches served as conduits for the global flow of ideas about love, marriage, gender, and sexuality during the mid-twentieth century.

---

2. Charrad and Goeken, "Continuity or Change," 42–45; Prazak, "Kenyan Families," 212.

Certainly, through their books, correspondence ministry, and marriage seminars, the Trobisches brought Western marital ideals to Africa. However, it is equally true that Walter's *J'ai Aimé Une Fille* and Ingrid's *The Joy of Being a Woman* brought African ideals to a Western audience. In *J'ai Aimé Une Fille*, readers learned about particular issues that young people faced during their quest to marry for love, such as the bride-price and the tradition of arranged marriage. And in *The Joy of Being a Woman*, readers learned how to live in harmony with the natural processes of the human body, a lesson Ingrid had first learned from the women in Tcholliré, Cameroon.

THE UNIQUENESS OF THE TROBISCHES IN THE HISTORY OF CHRISTIAN MISSION

The Trobisches believed marriage guidance was "a door for the gospel." They used marriage guidance to teach people about Christian theology and praxis. They invited people to confess sexual sins and then assured those people that their sins had been forgiven. They unpacked the meaning of Genesis 2:24 and adapted their particular illustrations of this verse to the context in which they were speaking. Over the course of their ministry, the Trobisches maintained that marriage guidance was not only *one* of many ways to spread the gospel, it was the *best* way to spread the gospel, given the confusion about sexuality in the modern world. "The family is the best landing place for the gospel," wrote Ingrid in her autobiography.[3]

During the 1970s, young people in both Africa and the United States tended to view Christian sexual ethics as either outdated or insufficient. In Africa, most young people knew the church opposed premarital sex, polygamy, and adultery, but they had yet to find a church elder who would help them think theologically about marrying for love, while also trying to balance parental expectations and the bride-price. In the United States, young people knew the church opposed premarital sex, but they rarely found someone who would give them concrete advice for how to remain chaste or how to recommit oneself to chastity if one had already become sexually active.

When Walter Trobisch published *J'ai Aimé Une Fille*, it was for many young people the first time that they had encountered a relevant and convincing rationale for premarital chastity. As a woman from Oregon wrote after reading *I Loved a Girl*, "Never before have my girl friends and I read anything on morals . . . that we have been fully interested in, moved by, and wanted to remember. We would each like a copy to share with our

3. Youngdale, *On My Way Home*, 15.

friends."[4] A pastor at a church in Addis Ababa where Trobisch delivered a lecture in 1967 expressed essentially the same sentiment when he said, "The fact that 'taboos' in the field of sex and marriage were studied in a Church in a reverent spirit was a major breakthrough for the Ethiopian Christian scene and a new revelation to the young who often feel that the Church maintains the basic realities shrouded in a mystery."[5]

Although the Trobisches conceived of their work as a way to introduce non-Christians to the faith, the people most affected by their work were those who already considered themselves Christian. Many of the letters the Trobisches received suggest that their books served as a catalyst for a kind of second conversion or recommitment to the core values of Christian faith. "Both of you—through your books—"The Joy of Being a Woman" and "I Loved a Girl" have made a very real impact on my life at a time when I was questioning many things and striving to understand what God had created us for in the male-female relationships," wrote a young woman to Ingrid.[6] She continued, "The wisdom and insight in your husband's book gave my husband and me the 'reason' to remain chaste before marriage." Young people were especially spurred to reform when they were personally counseled by Trobisch. Many young Africans and young Americans welcomed Trobisch's invitation to repent of their sexual sins, accepted his proclamation of forgiveness, and told him they planned to live out a new life in the power of the Holy Spirit.

The Trobisches were not unique in recognizing that Christianity has implications for sexuality and family life, nor were they unique in using sexual and marital practices to illustrate Christian teaching. However, they did have a remarkable ability to convey a Christian theology of love, sex, and marriage through story. Walter's *J'ai Aimé Une Fille*, as well as *My Beautiful Feeling* and several of the booklets in the "Here is My Problem" series,[7] used story to nudge readers towards premarital chastity, monogamy, spouse self-selection, and companionate marriage. The Trobisches were also unique in providing concrete, detailed guidance for some of the particular sexual and marital problems faced by people in mid-twentieth-century Africa and the West. As a woman speaking publicly about sex to mixed audiences in Africa, Ingrid was exceptional. And in trying to help clitoridectomized women to achieve orgasm, Walter was unique. The Trobisches were also some of the

---

4. W. and I. Trobisch to friends, September 1964, Missionary Personnel Files.

5. Ezra Gebremedhin, quoted in "Reactions and Echoes to Family Life Seminars," in W. and I. Trobisch to Morris Sorenson, 23 August 1971, Missionary Personnel Files.

6. H. D. to I. Trobisch, 21 January 1980, Ingrid Trobisch Papers.

7. *My Wife Made Me a Polygamist, The Person I Married Does Not Obey Me,* and *Can Sex Hurt Love?*

first Protestants to advocate the sympto-thermal method of Natural Family Planning, both in Africa and in the West.

The uniqueness of the Trobisches in the history of Christian mission also lies in the fact that they *as a couple* placed marital and sexual counseling *at the center* of their entire missionary life together. Most missionaries—even those who have been deeply attuned to the evangelistic potential of Christian family life—have put some other aspect of mission such as church work, medicine, school teaching, or Bible translation at the center of their work. The extent of the Trobisches' dedication to marriage guidance as "a door for the gospel" is therefore unusual in the history of Christian mission.

That the Trobisches decided to dedicate themselves to marriage counseling was due both to their own personal journey and to the circumstances of their time. The global reevaluation of sexual and marital practices during the mid-twentieth century created the need for marriage guidance. The Trobisches' experiences as missionaries in Tchollité and Libamba gave them the knowledge to develop a relevant message on marriage and sexuality. The East African Revival of the 1930s and 1940s and conversations within the International Missionary Council paved the way for the reception of the Trobisches' message in Africa. By the 1960s, the IMC, the All Africa Conference of Churches, and the Lutheran World Federation were all interested in supporting a Christian home movement. It was right at this time that the Trobisches were realizing the capacity of marriage guidance to spread the gospel and were publicizing this at conferences and in articles. In 1968, the LWF hired Walter to serve as Consultant on Family Counseling to the churches in Africa, thus enabling the Trobisches to reach a wider audience with their own particular take on African Christian marriage and to shape the overall Christian home movement in Africa. Lastly, just as the Trobisches were losing the backing of ecclesiastical organizations in Africa, InterVarsity Christian Fellowship in the United States began to sponsor their work among American college students. Thus, once again, both the needs of the moment—in this case, the struggle of evangelicals to respond to the sexual revolution—and the Trobisches' growing expertise in a Christian theology of sexuality facilitated their transition to marriage counseling in the United States. And, once again, they found they had a unique ability to contribute to the conversation about sexuality in the modern world.

CHRISTIAN FACILITATION OF A SHIFT TOWARDS SPOUSE SELF-SELECTION AND MARRYING FOR LOVE

The Trobisches were certainly unique in the history of Christian mission, but their story is also representative of the ways in which Christianity has helped to facilitate the global reevaluation of sexual and marital practices that took place during the twentieth century. There are far more people today marrying for love, pursing love within marriage, and seeing love as the point of marriage than there were a century ago.[8] Scholars have shown how this transition has been caused by industrialization, urbanization, modern forms of education, new conceptions of personhood, mass media, wage labor, family planning public health initiatives, longer life spans, and migration.[9] However, no single study has yet made an argument for the global impact of Christian mission on the global rise of spouse self-selection, marrying for love, and companionate marriage. Once we realize that the global shift to "love marriage" occurred during the very same time period when Christianity experienced a shift in its center of gravity from the northern to the southern hemisphere, it becomes important to probe the relationship between these two global shifts.[10] Such a project demands an entire book of its own (which I am currently working on), but for the time being let me use the Trobisches' story to hint at how the spread of Christianity has encouraged the global shift towards spouse self-selection and marrying for love.

Missionaries Modeled Marital Partnership

In chapter 1, we watched Ingrid and Walter Trobisch realize that putting their marriage on display could be a missionary strategy. As Ingrid remarked, "The fact that Walter and I could live together in love and harmony in our family was perhaps the first way that they [the people of Tcholliré] could believe [in Jesus]."[11] Walter carried around his new baby daughter with hopes that other men in the village would take note and begin to do likewise. Not all nineteenth- and twentieth-century missionary couples have been as intentional about modeling companionate marriage as the Trobisches, but most have shared the Trobisches' view that Christian marriage should be marked by love, intimacy, and partnership. Simply living out

---

8. Padilla, *Love and Globalization*, xv.

9. Hirsch and Wardlow, *Modern Loves*; Ahearn, *Invitations to Love*; Rebhun, *Heart Is Unknown Country*; Kendall, *Getting Married in Korea*.

10. Robert, "Shifting Southward."

11. I. Trobisch, Interview by Robert Shuster.

such marriages in the mission field helped to spread these ideals to places that had not yet encountered them or were in the process of encountering them because of social forces connected with modernization. This is not to say that romantic love and companionate marriage did not exist prior to the arrival of Christian missionaries in non-Christian lands, but rather that Christian missionaries have helped to cause "the companionate ideal [to grow] in prominence as part of the repertoire of concepts on which people draw when crafting their complicated lives."[12]

African Christians Valued Spouse Self-Selection and Companionate Marriage

We saw in chapters 2, 3, and 4 of this book that choosing a spouse and cultivating a companionate marriage were ideals often expressed by African Christians during the twentieth century. One of the many young women who corresponded by letter with Trobisch during the 1960s told him that she wanted to have "a good Christian family" and that she was going to "pray and beg God to help me find a real good lifemate."[13] Many others echoed her sentiments and demonstrated that they appreciated Trobisch's endorsement of spouse self-selection and companionate marriage. Cultivating companionate marriage was important to the *Balokole* of the East African Revival in the 1930s, '40s, and '50s. It was important to the All Africa Conference of Churches and the Association of Evangelicals of Africa and Madagascar in the 1960s and '70s. Both organizations issued statements on companionate marriage and urged churches to invest in marriage counseling.

The association of Christianity with spouse self-selection and companionate marriage has been observed in other contexts as well. According to Yung-Chung Kim, "the idea of equality between husband and wife gradually became accepted and practiced in Christian homes" in early-twentieth-century Korea.[14] In colonial India, converts used the nuclear model of family to set themselves apart from their non-Christian neighbors.[15] And in Papua New Guinea, couples have demonstrated their Christian faith by choosing to "live together, rather than in the separate men's and women's houses of

---

12. Wardlow and Hirsch, "Introduction," 6.
13. M. Bekele to W. Trobisch, 26 October 1967, Walter Trobisch Collection, Box 14, Folder B.
14. Kim, *Women of Korea*, 221.
15. Kent, *Converting Women*, 127.

the past."¹⁶ These couples use the notion that "God is love" to bolster their commitment to romantic love and companionate marriage.¹⁷ More research will have to be done to ascertain the extent to which spouse self-selection and companionate marriage have been bound up with Christianity in other contexts, but this data from Africa, Korea, India, and Papua New Guinea suggests that the correlation likely has wider resonance.

Schools, Churches, and Prayer

Schools founded by missionaries have given young people a place to meet someone of the opposite sex and have tended to cultivate individualism and the desire for personal choice in marriage. Church buildings and programs have also fostered spouse self-selection and marrying for love. We saw this play out with Kyereh, the young Ghanaian, who told Trobisch that he had met and fallen in love with a woman while singing in choir and participating in prayer meetings. Holly Wardlow has shown how churches in Papua New Guinea became a place for young people to meet each other, thus circumventing traditional avenues for the courtship process.¹⁸ A similar phenomenon was at work in early-twentieth-century Japan, where "the various services of the Church offer[ed] opportunities for young men and women to see each other and to become acquainted under wholesome conditions, something difficult to secure elsewhere."¹⁹ It is impossible to know how widespread has been the experience of falling in love at church, but we can certainly say that one of the unintended consequences of the spread of Christianity during the nineteenth and twentieth centuries has been that churches have given young people one more place to find and choose a spouse.

Not only the physical space of the church building, but also the spiritual space of prayer has bolstered the rise of spouse self-selection. We have seen the way in which young people who wrote to Trobisch were at times bewildered by their very desire to find and choose a spouse. In response, Trobisch proscribed prayer. Prayer helped young people feel less anxious about finding and choosing a spouse because it invited them to see God as the one ultimately responsible for guiding them through the dating process. And yet, prayer also allowed them to see themselves as involved in the process of finding a spouse. They could pray for God to lead them,

---

16. Wardlow and Hirsch, "Introduction," 1.
17. Wardlow, "All's Fair When Love Is War," 52.
18. Wardlow, "All's Fair When Love Is War," 65.
19. Speer et al., *Christian Home Making*, 105.

rather than passively waiting to receive an arranged spouse. Many of the same dynamics we find in the African letters to Trobisch were at work as Christianity and modernity spread in Asia, the Pacific, and Latin America. Young people in these contexts likely also felt alienated from their families, simultaneously excited and scared by the process of dating, anxious about choosing the right spouse. Prayer likely provided relief beyond the African context for Christian young people struggling to navigate the unfamiliar realm of dating in the modern world. In so doing, Christianity provided one more structure to support the rise of spouse self-selection and marrying for love.

WALTER TROBISCH'S DEATH AND THE END OF AN ERA

On October 13, 1979, Walter Trobisch died suddenly of a heart attack at the age of fifty-six.[20] Although Family Life Mission continued to engage in marriage guidance work after Walter's death and Ingrid went on to publish several books dealing with grief, femininity, and Christian identity, these topics are beyond the scope of this book.

Trobisch's death in 1979 marked the end of an era. For one thing, it corresponded with a declining interest in marriage guidance among mainline Christians in Africa. Marriage guidance had been a central concern of the All Africa Conference of Churches at its meetings in 1958 and 1963. During the late 1960s, the AACC had sponsored a series of Leadership Training Seminars on Marriage and Family Life. But by the late 1970s, most of the energy that had been directed toward marriage guidance was instead being directed toward ending the discrimination against women in church and society.[21]

Just as Trobisch's death can be seen as marking an end to the Christian home movement in Africa, so too it can be seen as marking the end of an era in the United States. During the 1960s and 1970s, there was room in American culture for the Trobisches' understanding of sexuality, which was a unique blend of feminist and conservative Christian ideals. Their middle-way perspective, however, was all but lost in the culture wars of the 1980s. Conservative evangelicals began arguing that "feminism" and "women in the work force" were two of the "forces of evil" that were "attacking the family."[22]

20. Youngdale, *On My Way Home*, 137–38.

21. All Africa Conference of Churches, *Engagement*, 104; All Africa Conference of Churches, *Follow Me, Feed My Lambs*, 27.

22. LaHaye, *Battle for the Family*, 28.

And secular feminists argued that religion was at best peripheral, and at worst antagonistic to the feminist project.[23] The space for people who wanted to try to hold feminist and Christian views together shrunk substantially, and evangelicals united around a "male headship" view of family.[24]

In the culture wars that continue to plague our modern world, the Trobisches' middle-way perspective deserves attention. Their message on love, sex, and marriage is not necessarily one to emulate today, but their method is. The Trobisches brought insights from different parts of the world to bear on a given question. They pursued a situational approach to counseling and attended to the importance of contextualizing the Christian faith. They were keen to highlight the importance of the cross; they weren't afraid of tragedy. It was this ability to push away fear, this willingness to embrace paradox, as much as their particular message about love, sex, and marriage, that enabled them to connect with so many people around the world and to shape the development of global, Christian sexual ethics.

---

23. This was evident in the fact that there was no sustained discussion of religion in the 383 pages of *Our Bodies, Ourselves*. If the church was mentioned, it was to show that the church was part of the problem (The Boston Women's Health Book Collective, *Our Bodies, Ourselves*, 184).

24. Stasson, "Politicization of Family Life," 106–21.

Bibliography

"Africa Family Counseling Consultant is Appointed." Clergy Biographical Files. Evangelical Lutheran Church in America Archives. Elk Grove Village, IL.

Ahearn, Laura M. *Invitations to Love: Literacy, Love Letters, and Social Change in Nepal.* Ann Arbor: University of Michigan Press, 2001.

All Africa Conference of Churches. *Engagement: The Second AACC Assembly Abidjan 69.* Nairobi: All African Conference of Churches, 1970.

———. *Follow Me, Feed My Lambs: Official Report, Fourth Assembly, All Africa Conference of Churches, Nairobi, Kenya, 2–12 August 1981.* Nairobi: Assembly Secretariat, AACC, 1982.

All-Africa Seminar on the Christian Home and Family Life. *The All-Africa Seminar on the Christian Home and Family Life.* Kitwe, Zambia: Geneva, 1963.

Anderson, Rufus. "Introductory Essay on the Marriage of Missionaries." In *Memoir of Mrs. Mary Mercy Ellis, Wife of Rev. William Ellis, Missionary to the South Seas,* edited by William Ellis, vii–xxii. Boston: Crocker & Brewster, 1836.

Anderson, Terry H. *The Movement and the Sixties.* New York: Oxford University Press, 1995.

Balmer, Randall. *Blessed Assurance: A History of Evangelicalism in America.* Boston: Beacon, 1999.

Banton, Michael. *West African City: A Study of Tribal Life in Freetown.* London: Oxford University Press, 1957.

Banyolak, Jean. "Africa Needs Marriage Counsellors." *All Africa Conference of Churches Bulletin* (February 1965) 68–69.

———. *My Wife Has Lost Interest in Sex.* Baden-Baden: Trobisch, 1967.

Beardsley, John. "Bill Gothard." *Biblical Discernment Ministries,* February 2004.

Billings, John. "The Quest: Leading to the Discovery of the Billings Ovulation Method." *Bulletin of Ovulation Method Research and Reference Centre of Australia* 29.1 (March 2002) 18–28.

The Boston Women's Health Book Collective. *Our Bodies, Ourselves: A Book By and for Women.* 2nd ed. New York: Simon and Schuster, 1979.

Bovet, Theodor. *Love, Skill and Mystery: A Handbook to Marriage.* New York: Doubleday, 1958.

Bowie, Fiona. "The Elusive Christian Family: Missionary Attempts to Define Women's Roles, Case Studies from Cameroon." In *Women and Missions: Past and Present,* edited by Fiona Bowie et al., 145–64. Providence, RI: Berg, 1993.

Bradley, Robert A. *Husband-Coached Childbirth.* New York: Harper and Row, 1965.

Breman, Christina Maria. *The Association of Evangelicals in Africa: Its History, Organization, Members, Projects, External Relations, and Message*. Zoetermeer, The Netherlands: Boekencentrum, 1996.
Callan, Hilary, and Shirley Ardener, eds. *The Incorporated Wife*. London: Croom Helm, 1984.
Charrad, Mounira M., and Allyson B. Goeken. "Continuity or Change: Family Law and Family Structure in Tunisia." In *African Families at the Turn of the 21st Century*, edited by Yaw Oheneba-Sakyi and Baffour K. Takyi, 27–48. Westport, CT: Praeger, 2006.
Chiabi, Emmanuel. *The Making of Modern Cameroon: A History of Substate Nationalism and Disparate Union, 1914–1961*. New York: University Press of America, 1997.
Christenson, Larry, and Nordis Christenson. *The Christian Couple*. Minneapolis: Bethany Fellowship, 1977.
Christiansen, Ruth. *For the Heart of Africa*. Minneapolis: Augsburg, 1956.
Comaroff, Jean, and John Comaroff. *Of Revelation and Revolution. Vol. 1: Christianity, Colonialism, and Consciousness in South Africa*. 2 vols. Chicago: University of Chicago Press, 1991.
Cone, Thomas E. *200 Years of Feeding Infants in America*. Columbus, OH: Ross Laboratories, 1976.
Coontz, Stephanie. *Marriage, a History: From Obedience to Intimacy or How Love Conquered Marriage*. New York: Viking, 2005.
The Couple to Couple League. "About CCL."
Davis, Rebecca L. *More Perfect Unions: The American Search for Marital Bliss*. Cambridge: Harvard University Press, 2010.
DeLancey, Mark Dike, et al. *Historical Dictionary of the Republic of Cameroon*. Fourth ed. Lanham, MD: Scarecrow 2010.
DeLancey, Mark W. *Cameroon: Dependence and Independence*. Boulder, CO: Westview, 1989.
Doherty, Mary A. *The Role of the African Woman*. London: Published for the World Federation of Catholic Young Women and Girls by the Africa Centre, [1962?].
The Educational Committee of the Augustana Foreign Missionary Society, ed. *The Missionary Calendar of the Augustana Foreign Missionary Society. Vol. 7: In His Name*. 9 vols. Rock Island, IL: Augustana Book Concern, 1927.
Epstein, Barbara Leslie. *The Politics of Domesticity: Women, Evangelism, and Temperance in Nineteenth-Century America*. Middletown, CT: Wesleyan University Press, 1981.
Epstein, Catherine A. *Nazi Germany: Confronting the Myths*. Chichester, UK: Wiley & Sons, 2015.
Erlank, Natasha. "Strange Bedfellows: The International Missionary Council, the International African Institute, and Research into African Marriage and Family." In *The Spiritual in the Secular: Missionaries and Knowledge About Africa*, edited by Patrick Harries and David Maxwell, 267–92 Grand Rapids: Eerdmans, 2012.
Ferdinando, Keith. "Byang Kato, 1936–1975." *International Bulletin of Missionary Research* 28.4 (2004) 169–74.
Finzsch, Norbert, and Marion Hulverscheidt. "Cliteridectomy." *Gender Forum* 67 (2018) 1–8.
Gandhi, Leela. *Postcolonial Theory*. New York: Columbia University Press, 1998.

Gebremedhin, Ezra. "The Nurture of the People of God." In *Addis Ababa: A Record of the Third All-Africa Lutheran Conference, Addis Ababa, Ethiopia, Oct. 12–21, 1965*, edited by Lutheran World Federation Dept. of World Mission, 61–70. Geneva: Lutheran World Federation, 1966.

Goode, William J. *World Revolution and Family Patterns*. New York: Free Press, 1963.

Goody, Jack, and Stanley J. Tambiah. *Bridewealth and Dowry*. Cambridge: Cambridge University Press, 1973.

Gordon, Mary Irwin. "How Does a Girl Decide?" *HIS* (May 1961) 4–6.

Grimshaw, Patricia. *Paths of Duty: American Missionary Wives in Nineteenth-Century Hawaii*. Honolulu: University of Hawaii Press, 1989.

Harmon, Linda. "Happy 60th Birthday Lamaze International! Happy Birthday to You!" https://www.lamaze.org/Connecting-the-Dots/Post/happy-60th-birthday-lamaze-international-happy-birthday-to-you-1#:~:text=This%20method%2C%20consisting%20of%20childbirth,gave%20birth%20assisted%-20by%20Dr.

Harris, Barbara J. *Beyond Her Sphere: Women and the Professions in American History*. Westport, CT: Greenwood, 1978.

Hastings, Adrian. *Christian Marriage in Africa*. London: SPCK, 1973.

Henry, Carl F. H. "A Time for Moral Indignation." *Christianity Today* 9.12 (March 12, 1965) 28–31.

Hirsch, Jennifer S., and Holly Wardlow, eds. *Modern Loves: The Anthropology of Romantic Courtship and Companionate Marriage*. Ann Arbor: University of Michigan Press, 2006.

Hunt, Keith, and Gladys Hunt. *For Christ and the University: The Story of Intervarsity Christian Fellowship-USA, 1940–1990*. Downers Grove, IL: InterVarsity, 1992.

Hunt, Nancy Rose. "Introduction." In *Gendered Colonialisms in African History*, edited by Nancy Rose Hunt et al., 1–15. Malden, MA: Blackwell, 1997.

Hunter, Jane. *The Gospel of Gentility: American Women Missionaries in Turn-of-the-Century China*. New Haven: Yale University Press, 1984.

Ingrid Trobisch Papers. David Trobisch Residence. Springfield, MO.

International Missionary Council. *The Missionary Obligation of the Church*. London: International Missionary Council, 1952.

Jewett, Paul K. *Man as Male and Female*. Grand Rapids: Eerdmans, 1975.

Johnson-Odim, Cheryl. "Actions Louder Than Words: The Historical Task of Defining Feminist Consciousness in Colonial West Africa." In *Nation, Empire, Colony: Historicizing Gender and Race*, edited by Ruth Roach Pierson and Nupur Chaudhuri, 77–93. Bloomington: Indiana University Press, 1998.

Joseph, Richard A. *Radical Nationalism in Cameroun: Social Origins of the U.P.C. Rebellion*. Oxford: Clarendon, 1977.

Justice, Keith. *Bestseller Index: All Books, by Author, on the Lists of Publishers Weekly and the New York Times Through 1990*. Jefferson, NC: McFarland, 1998.

Karanja, John. "Confession and Cultural Dynamism in the East African Revival." In *The East African Revival: History and Legacies*, edited by Emma Wild-Wood and Kevin Ward, 143–52. Kampala, Uganda: Fountain, 2010.

Kariuki, Obadiah. "Christian Home Life." In *The Church in Changing Africa: Report of the All-Africa Church Conference Held at Ibadan, Nigeria, January 10–19, 1958*. New York: International Missionary Council, 1958.

Karmel, Marjorie. *Thank You, Dr. Lamaze*. Philadelphia: Lippincott, [1959].

Kendall, Laurel. *Getting Married in Korea: Of Gender, Morality, and Modernity*. Berkeley: University of California Press, 1996.

Kent, Eliza F. *Converting Women: Gender and Protestant Christianity in Colonial South India*. Oxford: Oxford University Press, 2004.

Kibira, Josiah. "A Living Church in a Changing Society." In *Addis Ababa: A Record of the Third All-Africa Lutheran Conference, Addis Ababa, Ethiopia, Oct. 12–21, 1965*, edited by Lutheran World Federation Dept. of World Mission, 18–27. Geneva: Department of World Mission, 1966.

Kim, Yung-Chung. *Women of Korea: A History from Ancient Times to 1945*. Seoul: Ewha Womans University Press, 1979.

Kirkwood, Deborah. "Protestant Missionary Women: Wives and Spinsters." In *Women and Missions: Past and Present*, edited by Fiona Bowie et al., 23–42. Providence, RI: Berg, 1993.

Kitzinger, Sheila. *The Experience of Childbirth*. New York: International Publication Service, 1964.

Labode, Modupe. "From Heathen Kraal to Christian Home: Anglican Mission Education and African Christian Girls, 1850–1900." In *Women and Missions: Past and Present*, edited by Fiona Bowie et al., 126–44. Providence, RI: Berg, 1993.

LaHaye, Tim. *The Battle for the Family*. Old Tappan, NJ: Revell, 1982.

LaHaye, Tim and Beverly LaHaye. *The Act of Marriage: The Beauty of Sexual Love*. Grand Rapids: Zondervan, 1976.

Larsson, Birgitta. "Haya Women's Response to the East African Revival Movement." In *The East African Revival: History and Legacies*, edited by Kevin Ward and Emma Wild-Wood, 119–28. Kampala, Uganda: Fountain, 2010.

Larsson, Per. *Bishop Josiah Kibira of Bukoba: In an International Perspective*. Nairobi: Uzima, [1992].

Lawrence, Jeremy C. D. *The Iteso*. London: Oxford University Press, 1957.

Leavitt, Judith Walzer. *Brought to Bed: Child-Bearing in America, 1750–1950*. New York: Oxford University Press, 1986.

Le Vine, Victor T. "Cameroon (1955–1962)." In *Challenge and Response in Internal Conflict*, edited by Doris M. Condit and Bert H. Cooper. Washington, DC: American University, 1968.

The Life of the Church. Vol. 4, *The Madras Series*. 7 vols. New York: International Missionary Council, 1939.

Lindsay, D. Michael. *Faith in the Halls of Power: How Evangelicals Joined the American Elite*. New York: Oxford, 2009.

Little, Kenneth. "Attitudes Towards Marriage and the Family among Educated Young Sierra Leoneans." In *The New Elites of Tropical Africa*, edited by Peter C. Lloyd, 139–60. Oxford: Oxford University Press, 1966.

Lloyd, Peter C. *Africa in Social Change*. Harmondsworth, UK: Penguin, 1967.

Ludwig, Frieder. "Tambaram: The West African Experience." *Journal of Religion in Africa* 31.1 (2001) 49–91.

Mace, David R. *The Christian Response to the Sexual Revolution*. Nashville: Abingdon, 1970.

Mace, David R., and Vera Mace. *Marriage: East and West*. Garden City, NY: Doubleday, 1960.

Marie André du Sacré Cœur, Sister. *The House Stands Firm: Family Life in West Africa*. Milwaukee: Bruce, 1962.

Marsden, George. *Reforming Fundamentalism: Fuller Seminary and the New Evangelicalism.* Grand Rapids: Eerdmans, 1987.
Martin, William. *With God on Our Side: The Rise of the Religious Right in America.* New York: Broadway, 1996.
Masters, William H., and Virginia E. Johnson. *Human Sexual Response.* Boston: Little, Brown, 1966.
Mathews, Donald G., and Jane Sherron De Hart. *Sex, Gender, and the Politics of ERA.* New York: Oxford University Press, 1990.
Mathews, Winifred. *Dauntless Women: Stories of Pioneer Wives.* 1947. Reprint, Freeport, NY: Books for Library, 1970.
Mattson, Karl E. "A Soldier of the Cross." *The Lutheran Companion* (February 9, 1949) 7–8.
May, Elaine Tyler. *America and the Pill: A History of Promise, Peril, and Liberation.* New York: Basic, 2010.
Mba, Chuks J., and Martin W. Bangha. "Reflections on the Changing Family System in Cameroon." In *African Families at the Turn of the 21st Century*, edited by Yaw Oheneba-Sakyi and Baffour K. Takyi, 171–96. Westport, CT: Praeger, 2006.
Mbia, Guillaume Oyono. *Trois Prétendants . . . Un Mari.* Yaoundé, Cameroon: CLE, 1964.
Mbiti, John S. *African Religions and Philosophy.* New York: Praeger, 1970.
———. *Love and Marriage in Africa.* London: Longman, 1973.
Missionary Personnel Files. "Trobisch, Walter and Ingrid." Evangelical Lutheran Church in America Archives. Elk Grove Village, IL, 1957–1979.
Moena, Sylvia N. "Family Life in Soweto, Gauteng, South Africa." In *African Families at the Turn of the 21st Century*, edited by Yaw Oheneba-Sakyi and Baffour K. Takyi, 249–72. Westport, CT: Praeger, 2006.
Moffat, John S. *The Lives of Robert and Mary Moffat.* 12th ed. London: T. Fisher Unwin, 1925.
Mpolo, Masamba Ma. "Polygamy in Pastoral Perspectives." In *Families in Transition*, edited by Masamba Ma Mpolo and Cécile de Sweemer, 97–126. Geneva: WCC, 1987.
Nasimiyu-Wasike, Anne. "Polygamy: A Feminist Critique." In *The Will to Arise: Women, Tradition, and the Church in Africa*, edited by Mercy Amba Oduyoye and Musimbi R. A. Kanyoro, 101–18. Maryknoll, NY: Orbis, 1992.
Natural Family Planning International. "Not Just for Catholics." http://nfpandmore.org/notjustfor.shtml.
Nygard, Mark L. "Preaching in Rey Bouba: An Analysis of Its Call to Faith in Light of Luther's Church Postil." M.Th. thesis, Luther Northwestern Theological Seminary, 1988.
Oduyoye, Mercy Amba. *Daughters of Anowa: African Women and Patriarchy.* Maryknoll, NY: Orbis, 1995.
Oheneba-Sakyi, Yaw, and Baffour K. Takyi. "Introduction to the Study of African Families: A Framework for Analysis." In *African Families at the Turn of the 21st Century*, edited by Yaw Oheneba-Sakyi and Baffour K. Takyi, 1–25. Westport, CT: Praeger, 2006.
Padilla, Mark B. et al., eds., *Love and Globalization: Transformations of Intimacy in the Contemporary World.* Nashville: Vanderbilt University Press, 2007.

"Pastoral Counseling Held Great Need in Africa." *Religious News Service*, October 21, 1965.

Pauw, Berthold A. *The Second Generation: A Study of the Family among Urbanized Bantu in East London*. Cape Town, South Africa: Oxford University Press, 1963.

Payne, Roland. "Reactions and Echoes to Family Life Seminars." Missionary Personnel Files. Evangelical Lutheran Church in America Archives. Elk Grove Village, IL.

PBS. "The Pill." *American Experience*, 1999–2002. http://www.pbs.org/wgbh/amex/pill/timeline/timeline2.html.

Phillips, Arthur, ed. *Survey of African Marriage and Family Life*. London: Oxford University Press, 1953.

Plant, Rebecca Jo. *Mom: The Transformation of Motherhood in Modern America*. Chicago: University of Chicago Press, 2010.

Prazak, Miroslava. "Kenyan Families." In *African Families at the Turn of the 21st Century*, edited by Yaw Oheneba-Sakyi and Baffour K. Takyi, 197–226. Westport, CT: Praeger, 2006.

"A Protestant Affirmation on the Control of Human Reproduction." *Christianity Today* 13 (November 8, 1969) 18–19.

Rebhun, L. A. *The Heart Is Unknown Country: Love in the Changing Economy of Northeast Brazil*. Stanford, CA: Stanford University Press, 1999.

"Reports of Group I: Home and Family Life." In *The Church in Changing Africa: Report of the All-Africa Church Conference Held at Ibadan, Nigeria, January 10–19, 1958*, edited by Derrick Cuthbert, 26–29. New York: International Missionary Council, 1958.

Reyburn, William D. "My Pilgrimage in Mission." *International Bulletin of Missionary Research* 23.3 (1999) 117–19.

Robert, Dana L. *American Women in Mission: A Social History of Their Thought and Practice*. Macon, GA: Mercer University Press, 1997.

———. "The 'Christian Home' as a Cornerstone of Anglo-American Missionary Thought and Practice." In *Converting Colonialism: Visions and Realities in Mission History, 1706–1914*, edited by Dana L. Robert, 134–65. Grand Rapids: Eerdmans, 2008.

———. "Shifting Southward: Global Christianity Since 1945." *International Bulletin of Missionary Research* 24.2 (April 2000) 50–58.

Robinson, John A. T. *Honest to God*. Philadelphia: Westminster, 1963.

Roetzer, Josef. "The Sympto-Thermal Method: Ten Years of Change." *Linacre Quarterly* 45.4 (November 1978) 358–74.

Scanzoni, Letha. "The New Morality." In *The Marriage Affair: The Family Counselor*, edited by J. Allan Peterson, 241–46. Wheaton, IL: Tyndale, 1971.

———. *Sex and the Single Eye*. Grand Rapids: Zondervan, 1968.

———. *Sex Is a Parent Affair*. Glendale, CA: G/L, 1973.

———. *Why Wait? A Christian View of Premarital Sex* .Grand Rapids: Baker, 1975.

Scanzoni, Letha, and Nancy Hardesty. *All We're Meant to Be: A Biblical Approach to Women's Liberation*. Waco, TX: Word, 1974.

Schuyler, J. B. "Conceptions of Christianity in the Context of Tropical Africa: Nigerian Reactions to Its Advent." In *Christianity in Tropical Africa*, edited by Christian G. Baëta, 201–23. London: Oxford University Press, 1968.

Sharkey, Heather J. "Missionary Legacies: Muslim-Christian Encounters in Egypt and Sudan during the Colonial and Postcolonial Periods." In *Muslim-Christian Encounters in Africa*, edited by Benjamin F. Soares, 57–88. Leiden: Brill, 2006.

Slack, Alison T. "Female Circumcision: A Critical Appraisal." *Human Rights Quarterly* 10.4 (Nov. 1988) 437–86.

Small, Dwight. "Dating: With or Without Petting." *HIS* (November 1962) 15–23.

Smith, Edwin W. *The Mabilles of Basutoland*. London: Hodder and Stoughton, 1939.

Speer, Emma Bailey, et al. *Christian Home Making*. New York: Round Table, 1939.

Stasson, Anneke. "The Politicization of Family Life: How Headship Became Essential to Evangelical Identity in the Late Twentieth Century." *Religion and American Culture* 24.1 (Winter 2014) 100–38.

Stasson, Anneke Helen. "Love, Sex, and Marriage in the Global Mission of Walter and Ingrid Trobisch." Ph.D. diss., Boston University, 2013.

Stone, Lawrence. *The Family, Sex, and Marriage in England 1500–1800*. New York: Harper Colophon, 1977.

Sunquist, Scott, and Caroline N. Long. *History of Presbyterian Missions, 1944–2007*. Louisville, KY: Geneva, 2008.

Tone, Andrea. *Devices and Desires: A History of Contraceptives in America*. New York: Hill and Wang, 2001.

Trobisch, Ingrid Hult. Interview by Robert Shuster. Audio tape. 27 September 1988. Wheaton College. Billy Graham Center Archives. Collection 400.

———. *The Joy of Being a Woman . . . And What a Man Can Do*. San Francisco: Harper & Row, 1975.

———. *On Our Way Rejoicing*. Wheaton, IL: Tyndale, 1986.

Trobisch, Ingrid, and Elisabeth Roetzer. *An Experience of Love: Understanding Natural Family Planning*. Old Tappan, NJ: Revell, 1981.

———. *Mit Freuden Frau sein 2*. Wuppertal, Germany: Brockhaus, 1977.

Trobisch, Walter. "The Africa of Tomorrow Challenges Us." Walter Trobisch Collection. Evangelical Lutheran Church in America Archives. Elk Grove Village, IL.

———. "Attitudes of Some African Youth toward Sex and Marriage." *Practical Anthropology* 9.1 (1962) 9–14.

———. *Can Sex Hurt Love (Love is a Feeling to be Learned)?* Here Is My Problem 5. Baden-Baden: Trobisch, 1968.

———. "Church Discipline in Africa." *Practical Anthropology* 8.5 (1961) 200–6.

———. "Clitoridectomy in Its Relationship to Female Sexual Response as a Special Problem of Marriage Counselling in Africa." Walter Trobisch Collection. Box 13, Folder 16: Clitoridectomy Papers. Evangelical Lutheran Church in America Archives. Elk Grove Village, IL

———. *The Complete Works of Walter Trobisch*. Downers Grove, IL: InterVarsity, 1987.

———. "Congregational Responsibility for the Christian Individual." In *Third All-Africa Lutheran Conference in Addis Ababa, October 12–21, 1965*, edited by Lutheran World Federation Dept. of World Mission, 93–101. Geneva: Lutheran World Federation, 1966.

———. "Courtship without Dating: Marriage by the Installment Plan." Walter Trobisch Collection. Box 12. Folder 39. Evangelical Lutheran Church in America Archives. Elk Grove Village, IL.

———. *I Married You*. New York: Harper & Row, 1971.

———. *J'ai Aimé Une Fille: Une Correspondance Confidentielle*. 2nd ed. Karlsruhe, Germany: Karl Bauerle, 1963.

———. "The Leading Problem: Engagement." *World Christian Education*, Second Quarter (1963) 37–38.

———. *Love Is a Feeling to Be Learned*. Kehl/Rhein, West Germany: Trobisch, 1971.

———. *Love Yourself*. Downers Grove, IL: InterVarsity, 1976.

———. *My Beautiful Feeling*. Kehl/Rhein, West Germany: Trobisch, 1976.

———. *My Journey Homeward*. Ann Arbor, MI: Servant, 1986.

———. *My Wife Made Me a Polygamist*. Here Is My Problem 1. Kehl/Rhein, Germany: Trobisch, 1971.

———. *The Person I Married Does Not Obey Me*. Here Is My Problem 4. Baden-Baden: Trobisch, 1973.

———. "Pre-Marital Relations and Christian Marriage in Africa." *Practical Anthropology* 8.6 (1961) 257–61.

———. *Spiritual Dryness*. Don Mills, ON: InterVarsity, 1970.

———. "This Was Not Done in a Corner." Walter Trobisch Collection. Evangelical Lutheran Church in America Archives. Elk Grove Village, IL.

Trobisch, Walter, and David Trobisch. *The Adventures of Pumpelhoober in Africa, America and Germany*. St. Louis: Concordia, 1971.

Turner, John G. *Bill Bright and Campus Crusade for Christ: The Renewal of Evangelicalism in Postwar America*. Chapel Hill: University of North Carolina Press, 2008.

Walter Trobisch Collection. Evangelical Lutheran Church in America Archives. Elk Grove Village, IL.

Wardlow, Holly. "All's Fair When Love Is War: Romantic Passion and Companionate Marriage among the Huli of Papua New Guinea." In *Modern Loves: The Anthropology of Romantic Courtship and Companionate Marriage*, edited by Jennifer S. Hirsch and Holly Wardlow, 51–77. Ann Arbor: University of Michigan Press, 2006.

Wardlow, Holly and Jennifer S. Hirsch. "Introduction." In *Modern Loves: The Anthropology of Romantic Courtship and Companionate Marriage*, edited by Jennifer S. Hirsch and Holly Wardlow, 1–31. Ann Arbor: University of Michigan Press, 2006.

Weekes-Vagliani, Winifred. *Family Life and Structure in Southern Cameroon*. Paris: Development Centre of the Organisation for Economic Cooperation and Development, 1976.

Woloch, Nancy. *Women and the American Experience*. 2nd ed. New York: McGraw-Hill, 1994.

Youngdale, Ingrid Trobisch. *On My Way Home*. Bolivar, MO: Quiet Waters, 2002.

Zwelling, Elaine. "The History of Lamaze Continues: An Interview with Sunnye Strickland." *Journal of Perinatal Education* 10.1 (2001) 13–20.

www.ingramcontent.com/pod-product-compliance
Lightning Source LLC
Chambersburg PA
CBHW070917160426
43193CB00011B/1502